ESSENTIAL PSYCHOLOGY

General Editor
Peter Herriot

E5

MOTIVATION AT WORK

ESSENTIAL

A

B

C

D

E

F

PSYCHOLOGY

MOTIVATION AT WORK

Hywel Murrell

Methuen

To Ruth

First published in 1976 by Methuen & Co Ltd
11 New Fetter Lane, London EC4P 4EE
© 1976 Hywel Murrell
Printed in Great Britain by
Richard Clay (The Chaucer Press), Ltd
Bungay, Suffolk
ISBN (hardback) 0 416 84080 9
ISBN (paperback) 0 416 84090 6

We are grateful to Grant McIntyre of
Open Books Publishing Ltd
for assistance in the preparation of this series.

Contents

Acknowledgement

I would like to thank my wife and youngest daughter for carrying the main burden of running our farm during lambing to give me time to write this book. I would also like to thank Mrs Elizabeth Clarke who transcribed all the tapes. Leonard Neal presented a paper at the fiftieth anniversary celebration of the National Institute of Industrial Psychology which started the train of thought which has led to this book; for this I am also grateful.

Editor's Introduction

The relationship between psychological theory and the application of psychology in the work situation is not a simple one. In the area of motivation at work, it is murky in the extreme. In this fascinating historical review, Hywel Murrell traces the fads and fashions in the use management has made of the psychology of motivation. He suggests that a major objective of management has always been control, with the means of control shifting from financial to psychological incentives and threats. He concludes that whether carrots and sticks or self-actualization are the currently favoured model, the real determinants of managerial practice are the social, political, and economic climate of the period.

Unit E of *Essential Psychology* deals with a particular area of applied psychology; psychology and work. This is an ideal topic to demonstrate the ways in which the different psychological models of man and their associated findings can be utilized. The human being as a processor of information copes with varied inputs in his job and has to adjust his behaviour accordingly. As a social being, he is much affected by the groups of people with whom he works and the organization within which he operates. As a developing person, his changing view of himself will partly consist of his view of himself at work. As an individual, he brings differing skills and motives to his work. Above all, as a human being, he possesses the capacity to change his work situation to suit his own abilities and objectives.

Essential Psychology as a whole is designed to reflect this changing structure and function of psychology. The authors are both academics and professionals, and their aim has been to introduce the most important concepts in their areas to beginning students. They have tried to do so clearly but have not attempted to conceal the fact that concepts that now appear central to their work may soon be peripheral. In other words, they have presented psychology as a developing set of views of man not as a body of received truth. Readers are not intended to study the whole series in order to 'master the basics'. Rather, since different people may wish to use different theoretical frameworks for their own purposes, the series has been designed so that each title stands on its own. But it is possible that if the reader has read no psychology before, he will enjoy individual books more if he has read the introductions (A1, B1, etc.) to the units to which they belong. Readers of the units concerned with applications of psychology (E, F) may benefit from reading all the introductions.

A word about references in the text to the work of other writers – e.g. 'Smith (1974)'. These occur where the author feels he must acknowledge an important concept or some crucial evidence by name. The book or article referred to will be listed in the References (which double as Name Index) at the back of the book. The reader is invited to consult these sources if he wishes to explore topics further.

We hope you enjoy psychology.

Peter Herriot

I
Introduction

A satisfied need is not a motivator of behaviour! This is a fact of profound significance. McGregor.

This book will be rather different from the others in the series in that it will be dealing very largely with activities which have been carried out by people other than psychologists. It is true that some psychologists have studied and written about motivation as it affects industry and have even experimented on the shop floor, but on the whole the ideas and activities which will be reported upon herein have emanated mainly from industrial management within industry itself, with some help from researchers and others with affiliations to sociological or management departments in universities. This does not mean that psychologists should not be very well aware of what has been happening over very nearly the last hundred years, since developments have followed a fairly logical sequence and anyone wishing to involve himself in the industrial scene must be conversant with what has gone before, whatever its origin.

There are many words which are used in a variety of senses and which convey a variety of ideas. An 'upset' means one thing to a mechanical engineer, another to a chemical engineer and something quite different to a physician. Even 'vigilance', the darling of the experimental psychologist, means one thing to the physiologist, another thing to the psychologist and yet something completely different to the industrialist. The situation becomes even worse when the word represents a fairly woolly concept, such as 'fatigue' or 'boredom', which is difficult to define and almost impossible to measure and which may mean one thing to one man and something different again to the next. 'Motivation' undoubtedly comes into this class; we all think we know what it means but when we are asked to define it or measure it we find ourselves at a loss. It is not surprising therefore that management has one idea, some social scientists another and that psychologists cannot even agree amongst themselves (see D2). Why if the situation is so indeterminate, you may ask, is a book on motivation and work included in a series on essential psychology? The reason is quite simple; our level of prosperity and our level of well-being all depend upon everyone, whatever job they are in, doing their job to the best of their capacity and ability – on them being 'motivated', whatever this may be. It is undoubtedly true that even after more than one hundred years' effort we have not really got very much further than seeing a gleam of light at the end of a tunnel. The whole field is crying out for attention by occupational psychologists with their special interest in the individual rather than in the mass. But anyone who gets himself involved must clearly know something of the background, the natural history if you like, and of the efforts, both sophisticated and unsophisticated, which have been made to achieve motivation at work. It is this background which this book attempts to give, with perhaps a sneaking hope that some of those who read it may become sufficiently excited to get involved themselves.

Management's efforts to find the determinants of motivation and performance in industry, whether these efforts are from line managements or from management scholars, have been primarily in terms of incentives or inducements. They seem to be very little in doubt that these are needed, but it is when they come to have a start to decide what form they should take that the difficulties really commence. Academic psychologists see the subject very differently, in terms of drives and needs and so on; these will not be dealt with in

10

detail since they are covered more fully elsewhere in the series (see D2, A3). Applied psychologists have interpreted these basic ideas in a variety of different ways. One group developed theories in fairly classical terms of human *needs and drives* (e.g. Maslow, 1954). Another group, led by Gestalt psychologists, have stressed that perception is the only basic determinant of behaviour because it ultimately determines the manner in which people will respond to their needs (Patterson, 1964). Finally, a group have developed the line, which is also widely accepted by personnel management in industry, that performance can only be understood in terms of an individual's ability (e.g. Vroom, 1964).

Although we can say with hindsight that management's efforts to induce their employees to produce more were, in effect, motivating them, management itself until very recently did not seem to recognize motivation as a concept. Actually, so far as management is concerned, 'motivation' was simply a phase in a series of fashions in management which have been explored in the thirty odd years since the end of World War Two. That these fashions should have been thought to have been worth exploring at all is largely due to a radical change in industry since the end of the war. Right from the darkest ages of slavery and serfdom, up to the end of the 1930s, labour was considered to be a commodity, and an expendable commodity at that, which could be bought and sold in the market place. The basic ethic was one of punishment; the slave was told 'if you don't do as I say you will be whipped', whereas the Georgian factory worker was told 'if you don't obey me you will be sacked'. Of course the factory worker knew perfectly well that if his output was good and efficient then his livelihood would not be at risk, so in practice the threat lost some of its force; an employer could not afford to loose good, skilled men even during the depression, but he always had dismissal as the ultimate sanction should an employee become too 'cussed'.

After the war things changed. A new generation of better educated and more sophisticated work-people became available, who because of social security, were prepared to argue the toss and damn the consequences. Moreover, they became

11

more organized both into small work groups and into larger unions, so management was no longer dealing with individuals. This continued post-war a change which was already happening in the inter-war years. Thus although management could still imagine that it was using some kind of punishment sanction by the manipulation of monetary rewards their efforts were largely nullified by action on the part of the workers. Because they now had to coerce rather than drive, management had to change its ideas and its management style. But it is indeed ironic that at a time when management is becoming conscious of the need to consider and to consult with its employees, their efforts should be rewarded by virtually a static rate of production and a larger number of strikes than ever before in our industrial history.

Because of this change it is convenient to take 1939 as the end of one era, but also the commencement of another which has continued until the present time. Thus, we can look at the work which has been done in two parts with 1939 as the dividing line and each part in turn will be sub-divided into those things which industry has done and those things which have been done primarily by those outside industry, and this normally means in the universities or in the management schools.

Before World War Two management efforts were mainly concentrated on incentives. In the Victorian period and up to about 1919 payment was almost invariably by piece-work. The idea of guaranteeing a minimum weekly wage and paying the remainder by means of a bonus was developed in the 1880s and 90s but was popularized by Charles Bedaux, and his system and its derivatives were the main alternatives to straight piece-work up to the Second World War. Less well known and widely used were the earlier systems of Gantt, Halsey, Rowan and others. The main alternative to these bonus systems was straight piece-work. A differential piece-work had been proposed by F. W. Taylor as part of his concept of scientific management but neither this, nor Merricks' alternative version, seemed to have had any very great following.

The turn of the century saw the birth of motion study

with Frank Gilbreth as the midwife. It is difficult now to discover from what has been written whether Gilbreth's main concern was primarily to cut costs without increasing the work load, or whether he had in mind improvement of worker motivation as a result of more efficient and orderly methods of work. This latter may well be so since his wife, Lillian (mother of his 'cheaper by the dozen' children), was a psychologist, but it must be remembered that it was not until more than two decades later that the Hawthorne research suggested that careful attention to a job was of itself a motivator (see p. 55).

There appears to have been only a comparatively small amount of industry-inspired research in the pre-1939 period. That which is almost certainly the most widely known was carried out at the Hawthorne Works of the Western Electric Company in Chicago between 1924 and 1932 (Roethlisberger and Dickson, 1939). The first two and a half years of research were occupied in experiments on illumination, and it was the outcome of these experiments which caused the work to continue from 1927 to 1932 in a study of the various factors which contributed to employee effectiveness within the general context of human relations. It is true that the word motivation does not appear in the index to Roethlisberger and Dickson's book, but it is equally clear from their statement of the problem that they were studying employee motivation in the sense that industry tends to understand this term. The Hawthorne experiments cut across the boundaries between industry and academia; the main inspiration in the organization of the experiments seems to have come from within the company itself but there were a number of academics, notably Elton Mayo, who were deeply involved in planning and evaluating the studies and also probably provided much of the drive to keep the work going.

In Britain the main research-associated studies were carried out by the Industrial Fatigue Research Board (IFRB), subsequently renamed the Industrial Health Research Board (IHRB), which was controlled by the Medical Research Council (MRC). Their activities were conducted almost entirely within industry itself and were very wide-ranging, covering, inter alia, hours of work, rest pauses, dexterity tests, accidents, atmospheric conditions, vision and lighting, time and motion study, work methods, posture and physique, absenteeism, vocational guidance and selection. Very closely related to the IFRB was the National Institute of Industrial Psychology (NIIP) whose work was also in its early days based on the shop floor; its publications in the first five years of the journal of the NIIP from 1922 to 1927 covered such things as the introduction of rest pauses, investigation into the packing of chocolates and into breakages, investigations in a coal mine, in a cabinet factory, in the textile industry, in an engineering works, the assembly and repair of gas stoves and fires, and conditions on farms. Writing in 1958 Eric Farmer, who was one of the first people to join Charles Myers at the launching of the NIIP, said 'The principles (were) to ease the effort required by the worker and not to endeavour to increase output by other incentives. It was always found that output increased when some of the hinderances to effectiveness had been removed by adjusting the work more closely to the natural capacity of the worker.' Here we have the beginning of a suggestion that there could be non-financial incentives, that workers could be motivated by something other than money.

Also, during the period, attitude surveys made their appearance although nowadays little is heard about what was done at that time. Even at that early date the validity of the technique was being questioned; LaPiere (1934) reported that the opinions and intentions revealed in a survey bore very little relationship to actual behaviour. Even before the First World War some psychologists were beginning to show an interest in the industrial scene. For instance in 1913 Münsterberg published a book on psychology and industrial efficiency in which he proposed that there were industrial activities which could be promoted by psychological techniques and these included the selection of the best possible workers, establishment of the best possible psychological conditions for effective work and, in rather a more different sphere, influencing behaviour through advertising and salesmanship! Some books on industrial psychology had been published but they were

14

largely concerned with the techniques of selection and training.

When World War Two was over and industrial activity was resumed, the climate was very different from what it had been before, with the controls and sanctions which management had been accustomed to use no longer viable. Some substitute had to be found and management grabbed at anything which appeared to offer promise. So the last thirty years have been characterized by a series of fashions following one after the other with management jumping aboard usually without clearly knowing what they were doing, and then after a time jumping off when something more promising hove in sight.

So first there was joint consultation; which was really nothing very new since generally half-hearted and largely unsuccessful efforts had been made in this direction throughout the inter-war period. This had hardly got off the ground when the golden age of incentives was ushered in, pushed along by industrial consultants who had got to find something else to do now that their wartime activities were over, by the commercial exploitation of predetermined motion-time systems (PMTS), also often called synthetics, and by the change of name of pre-war 'Time and Motion Study' to 'Work Study' by Currie at ICI. A not unusual consequence of the introduction of financial incentives was that management increasingly withdrew from many of its responsibilities *vis-à-vis* the men on the shop floor, under the impression that if you bribed them to work there was no longer any need to lead them; thus it became the workers' responsibility to ensure that work ran efficiently. Throughout this period there was a development which had started in the inter-war years and which was rapidly accelerating, namely the build-up of larger and smaller groups which would corporately resist management's attempts to increase productivity. So management was no longer in a position to motivate *individuals* since it was not individuals but groups which decided what the rate of production was going to be. Thus attention switched to group motivation and productivity bargaining became all the rage round about 1960. But before this happened, there was one last kick in the idea that you could motivate individuals when

15

training was for a short time considered to be the fashionable thing to do.

Productivity bargaining proved to be one of the final acts in motivation by financial reward, a movement which had held the stage for more than eighty years. Bonuses continued, and still continue even now, to be the main method of payment but the inefficiency of the methods of setting the price for the job, the bargaining power of the unions, and the setting of norms of production by individual work groups has turned these payment methods into powerful disincentives. Then for the first time the word 'motivation' began to appear, coupled with the idea that there were non-financial incentives which could be even more important than the financial ones, and for the first time management's ideas were really being influenced by psychologists and others in the behavioural sciences such as Herzberg or Maslow. Others such as Likert, McGregor or Vroom directed attention to management itself and to the proposition that if the shop floor appeared to be lacking in motivation and effort, the first place to seek for the causes was in the front office. Thus from the one group came ideas for job enlargement and so on, while from the other came the concept of a management style. This phase is now rapidly waning and industry is looking for something else to put in its place. A group of psychologists in government service has developed the concept of 'the quality of working life', while others are pushing the idea that emphasis on the importance of the social aspect of industry will develop as an important motivator in the last quarter of the twentieth century. Yet another group feel that it is the study of behaviour in organizations which is going to show the way for the future.

A major feature of the post-war period has been the change, particularly in the late fifties and the early sixties, from industry going it alone to industry getting more and more involved in the application of ideas which have come from research by academics. In a sense, industry has squeezed itself dry of ideas and is now frantically grasping at anything that looks promising; but it must be said that clear examples of successful implementation of the ideas put forward by the academics are rather hard to find; there still seems to be too large a gap between the shop floor and the ivory tower and for many the lift seems to have stuck half way down, as it were, at the management level rather than going down to the basement where all the action is.

The change in management's relationships with the shop floor has been accompanied by other changes just as far reaching. Educational advantages have greatly increased. Squalor and poverty have given way to comparative affluence, the bicycle has given way to the motor car as the popular means of transport, Benidorm has replaced Brighton or Blackpool as the mecca for the holidaymaker during a Wakes week, or fortnight as it has now become. To anyone who lived through the depression of the thirties, the affluence of the fifties and the sixties must seem like the millennium. But, actually, the period has been one of escalating strikes, of increasing bitterness, or insubordination and bloody-mindedness and, worst of all, of steadily declining relative efficiency. In spite of all management's attempts to provide incentives to work hard and well, there seems to be an increasing inclination, backed by group action to do exactly the opposite. To quote Leonard Neal (1971) 'yet these same people, who bring so little enthusiasm to the work that provides them and their families with their standard of life, can, in other circumstances, apply themselves enthusiastically to the most unrewarding tasks. People will work without pay in trade union branches, political parties, youth clubs, church activities. They diligently fling themselves under decaying old motor cars on Saturday mornings while on Sundays they cultivate gardens and allotments to produce the most expensive vegetables you can imagine. When not engaged in these tasks, they are either eagerly watching dangerous football matches in appalling weather conditions, or sitting for endless hours in the cold and damp by depressing rivers and canals, fishing for unenthusiastic and inedible fish.' Something has obviously gone seriously wrong and nobody really has any clear idea of what should be done to put things right. Neither side of industry has yet begun to learn how to live in an industrial society without the sanctions which

17

were formerly available which enabled management to manage by enforcing its will upon the shop floor. There are signs of a move towards worker participation in the decision-making processes of a concern at all levels; at the time this book is being written workers' cooperatives are very much in the news. Whether the workers who are involved will have sufficient motivation to make these ventures a success, or whether the old habits of what F. W. Taylor calls 'soldiering' will still persist have yet to be resolved. Time alone will tell.

We have looked very briefly, by way of setting the scene, at the wide range of techniques which industry has used in order to motivate its work-people to work harder and more efficiently. It is indeed ironical that the more management has moved away from the punitive approach towards consultation and collaboration the less well motivated have the work-people seemed to become.

2
Motivation by management – pre-1939

In the latter part of the industrial revolution management's idea of motivating its workers was the use of fear and financial incentives. The first was exercised by the threat of dismissal and the latter by paying piece-work – the more you make the more you earn. It is unlikely that in those early days management even thought in terms of 'motivation'. The objective was high production and the methods were traditional and unquestioned. It was not until 1954 that Morris Viteles, Professor of Psychology at the University of Pennsylvania, in publishing *Motivation and Morale in Industry* slotted financial incentives into the overall picture of motivators. Fear was still about, particularly during the slump, but it was usually not used in the same punitive way as before.

The origins of incentive wage schemes are lost in the mists of antiquity. It has been suggested that as far back as 400 BC the Chaldeans operated such a scheme, but the direct precursor of more modern piece-work systems was the development of 'home' work in the sixteenth century when material was supplied by an employer who paid for the work done by the piece. When work was transferred to the factory the same system was normally retained, although there were some scattered attempts to employ some kind of incentive in the form of a bonus (Lipson, 1948). Any kind of measurement aimed at determining what the piece-work rates should be was apparently completely absent; the amount paid per piece was dependent on estimates based on past work which were largely a matter of bargaining and trial and error. All this began to change in about 1880 when Frederick Taylor began a systematic study of management techniques with the object of developing methods of task improvement and task measurement from which more equitable and realistic targets for production could be established. It was this emphasis on measurement which caused Taylor to describe his new approach as 'scientific management'.

Scientific Management

Frederick Winslow Taylor was born in 1856 in Philadelphia to a middle-class family. His parents wished him to become a lawyer, so they sent him to the Phillips Exeter Academy to prepare for the Harvard entrance examination. He came top of his class in the Academy but his vision was so impaired, allegedly, because of excessive study by the light of a paraffin lamp, that he was advised not to continue study at Harvard. So in 1874 he was apprenticed as a pattern maker and machinist in a small shop in Philadelphia. In 1878 he became a journeyman pattern maker and almost immediately moved to the Midvale Steel Company as an ordinary labourer. In the succeeding eight years he worked his way through being a time-keeper, a machinist, gang boss, foreman and finally assistant engineer to the chief engineer of the works. He obtained the ME degree at Stephens Institute by part-time study. It was during the latter part of this period that he started the development of ideas for which he has become famous, or notorious according to your point of view. Copley, in his biography of Taylor, says that when he was first introducing his ideas as a young foreman he was 'frequently threatened with violence, and the fight increased in bitterness; the men resorting to such things as the deliberate breaking of machines and their foremen to large scale fining and firing.'

It was not until 1895 that Taylor presented his ideas to the world in a paper entitled 'A piece-rate system, being a step towards partial solution of labor problems' which he presented at the Detroit meeting of the American Society of Mechanical Engineers. In this paper, he describes a system of management which he had introduced at the Midvale Steel Company and which had operated successfully (or so he claimed) for more than ten years. It consisted of three principle elements: an elementary rate-fixing system, a differential rate system of piece-work and a method of managing men who work by the day. By 'elementary' he did not mean something simple, but the breaking down of a work task into its elements. This word is not used now but because that is what Taylor called it, it will be used in this discussion.

Elementary rate-fixing involved the careful study of the time required to do each of the elementary operations into which the task may be divided. These are then classified, recorded and indexed and when a piece-work price is required, the job is divided into its elementary operations and the time required to do each job is found from the records and the total time for the job is summed from these data. In developing this method Taylor anticipated by sixty years the later development of what have become known as 'synthetics' or predetermined motion time systems (PMTS) which are being sold commercially under such names as Methods Time Measurement (MTM) or Work Factor.

The differential rate system consisted in offering two different rates for the same job. A high price is established for each piece when the work is finished in what Taylor describes as 'the shortest possible time and in perfect condition'; a lower price is paid if it takes a longer time to do the job or if any of the work is defective. This system therefore requires that production targets should be set and, if these targets are met, the piece-work rate will be higher, usually by 50 per cent, than the rate when these criteria are not met. Thus when what Taylor calls 'a first-class man' meets his target he not only is paid because he has produced more, but is paid at a higher rate, whereas the converse is true of the man who cannot meet the target.

Taylor's system of managing men who are on day-work consists in paying men and not positions – a forerunner of

21

merit rating. Thus each man's wages are fixed according to the skill and energy with which he performs his work and not according to the position which he fills. But this involves keeping systematic and careful records of the performance of each man as to his punctuality, attendance, integrity, rapidity, skills and accuracy and from time to time the wages paid to him are readjusted in accordance with this record. Taylor claimed that when men are paid according to the position they fill and not according to their individual character, energy, skill and reliability, the ambitious men soon conclude that since there is no profit in their working hard the best thing for them to do is to work as little as they can and still keep their position. He goes on to point out that if men are herded together into classes regardless of personal character and performance, the proper and legitimate answer is the formation of a labour union and the holding of strikes, either to increase the rate of pay and to improve conditions of employment or to resist the lowering of wages and other encroachments on the part of the employers. Taylor claimed that when men are paid and not positions there is no need for the men to be unionized. Taylor's obvious feeling that the unions tend to sour the relationships of a good employer and his work-people recurs in most of his writings and cannot have endeared him to the unions.

Taylor's next excursion into print was in 1903 when he presented a paper entitled 'Shop Management'. This paper appears to have been received just as coolly as was its predecessor; in it he deals rather less with the problems of setting piece-work rates and rather more with the selection and training of the work-force. He believed profoundly in the importance of money as a motivator and his selection consisted in trying to identify 'first-class men' on the grounds that first-class man can do from between two to four times as much work as can be done by an average man. This he claimed was not known either to employers or to the workmen. The potentialities of a first-class man are related to the pace of work which he can keep up for a long term of years without injury to his health. Taylor believes that under these circumstances men will become happier and will thrive provided they are paid up to 100 per cent more than the average in their trade.

We see for the first time the suggestion that there should be an allowance for rest and for accidental or unavoidable delays. And he even went so far as to experiment with the reduction of working hours and the introduction of rest pauses, thereby anticipating by thirty years the efforts of the Industrial Fatigue Research Board.

Taylor gives an account of a study which he carried out on girls who were inspecting ballbearings which showed that the girls spent much of their time in partial idleness, talking, working intermittently or doing absolutely nothing (Murrell found exactly the same thing still going on in the 1960s). Their hours of work were reduced from ten and a half per day to eight and a half and in addition instead of having to work the whole of Saturdays, they were given a half day which even further reduced the total hours worked. Two breaks of ten minutes each were given in the middle of the morning and the afternoon, during which the girls were expected to leave their place of work and were allowed to talk; but otherwise, talking was prevented by moving them so far apart that talking became impossible. The shorter hours and improved conditions made it possible for the girls really to work steadily during the work period instead of pretending to work. Differential piece-work was introduced and the work of each girl was carefully measured each hour and they were informed whether they were keeping up with their tasks or how far they had fallen short of their targets; an assistant was sent by the foreman to encourage those who were falling behind and to help them catch up. The final result of the changes in the inspection department was that 35 girls did the work which had previously been done by 120, their pay was doubled and they were working shorter hours. There was a big improvement in the quality of the work. The reduction in the number of girls was achieved not only because of the improvement in the working conditions, but also because lazy and unpromising girls were weeded out and more ambitious ones were substituted. And here again we see Tayolr's preoccupation with ensuring that he employed only what he called high-price or first-class individuals.

In order to achieve this end he instituted what was probably one of the first systematic selection procedures. He lists the qualities which go to make what he calls a 'well-rounded' man, which were brains, education, special or technical knowledge, manual dexterity or strength, tact, energy, grit, honesty, judgement or common sense and good health. There are plenty of men who possess only three of these qualities and who could be hired at any time for a labourer's wage, but with four of these qualities you get a higher-priced man. Men combining five of these qualities may be hard to find and those with seven or eight, are almost impossible to get.

Taylor discusses at length the qualities required for a foreman and it is interesting to note that consideration for the men working under him is not one of the things which is included. He is however, expected to be a hustler, a man of energy, and be able to set a good example to the men working for him. He claims that it is virtually impossible to get anybody with all the qualities which he lists and therefore he devised what he called *functional management*. This consisted in dividing the responsibilities of the shop-floor management so that each man from the assistant superintendent down to foreman should be confined to the performance of a single leading function. The effect of this on the operatives themselves is that instead of receiving their instructions from just one man, they may get orders and help directly from up to eight, each of whom is performing his own particular function. He contrasts this with what he calls the military type chain of command which was so strongly entrenched in the owners and management of industry at that time and, it may be said, since. His ideas of the proper functioning of management were so entrenched in the Midvale management that it was not until years after his functional management had been in continual use that he dared tell his superiors about it.

Discipline he considered to be of great importance and he believed that one of the members of the management team under functional management system should be known as the shop disciplinarian! He gives advice on how to deal with certain men who are 'thick-skinned' and 'coarse-grained' and who are apt to mistake a mild manner and a kindly way for timidity and weakness. With such men the severity both of words and manner should be gradually increased until either the desired result has been obtained or the possibilities of the English language have been exhausted. In order to discipline a man you can do one of four things. You can lower his wages, you can lay him off, you can fine him or you can give him a series of black marks which when they reach a pre-determined total can result in one of the former things happening. On the whole he believed it undesirable actually to sack somebody as a disciplinary action. This approach of Taylor is a clear example of the punishment situation in industry before 1939. If any manager tried to do these things now, he would have an empty factory almost before he had time to blink!

Finally, in his paper Taylor gives in great detail the method of carrying out time studies, the first description of the technique which has become so much a part of the industrial scene ever since.

As time went on and Taylor's ideas became more widely applied, they raised a great deal of controversy and opposition. It was at a hearing before an Inter-state Commission in 1909 that the label 'scientific management' was first openly used and this had such news value that it roused intense public interest. Actually, Taylor did not himself coin the term; this is credited to Louis D. Brandeis who was one of Taylor's most ardent supporters and a kind of self-appointed public relations man. He went on later to become a Supreme Court Justice.

The principal objective of scientific management is to secure the maximum prosperity for the employer coupled with the maximum prosperity for each employee. For the employee, this means not only higher wages but the development of each man to a state of maximum efficiency so that he may be able to do the highest grade of work for which his natural abilities fit him. Wherever possible, he should be given this kind of work to do. Scientific management also means that measurements should be used rather than guess-work, and Taylor describes a scientific investigation into what he calls the accurate study of the motives which influence men, which he considered at first to be a matter for individual observation and judgement and not a proper subject for exact scientific experiment. Exactly what the experiments were we are not told, but he seems to have believed that he had derived some laws which owing to the fact that a very complex organism – the human being – is being experimented with, are subject to a larger number of exceptions than is the case with laws relating to material things. Yet he is quite sure that laws of this kind unquestionably exist and that clearly defined, they can be of great value as a guide in dealing with workmen. All that is actually quoted as the outcome of this research is the use of a task or stint which, together with a guaranteed bonus, constitute two important elements of the mechanism of scientific management.

As has already been mentioned Taylor's activities and those of others following his ideas aroused a good deal of antagonism particularly amongst the unions for which Taylor obviously felt a good deal of antipathy. The upshot was that a special committee of the House of Representatives was set up to investigate 'the Taylor and other systems of shop management' which started its investigations in January 1912. It is in the transcript of his testimony before this committee that we perhaps get the clearest statement of what he really feels he is trying to achieve.

Taylor began his evidence by disclaiming that his system was in fact called the 'Taylor system' and insisting on using throughout the term 'scientific management'. He listed at length the things which scientific management is not. 'It is not an efficiency device, it is not a system of figuring costs, a system of paying men, a piecework system, a bonus system, a premium system, it is not a motion study.' What it is and what it involves is a complete mental revolution on the part of working men as to their duty towards their work, towards their fellow men and towards their employers. It involves an equally complete mental revolution on the part of management, the foreman, superintendents, the owners of the business, the boards of directors and so on, as to their duties towards their fellow workers in management, towards their working men and towards all their daily problems 'and without this complete mental revolution on both sides, scientific management does not exist.' The main problem between managers and workers is the division of the surplus accruing from their efforts, that is, how much goes in dividends and how much goes in increased pay. Both sides argue over this and gradually they come to look upon each other as antagonists and at times even as enemies. The mental revolution requires that both sides take their eyes off the division of the surplus as the all-important matter and turn their attention towards increasing the size of the surplus. Then it becomes so large that it is unnecessary to quarrel over how it should be divided. Managers and workers should come to see that when they stop pulling against each other and instead both turn and push shoulder to shoulder in the same direction, the size of the surplus created by their joint efforts is truly astounding. They should both realize that when they start to substitute friendly cooperation and mutual help for antagonism and strife, they are together able to make this surplus so enormously greater than it was in the past that there is ample room for a large increase in wages for the workmen and an equally great increase in profits for the management. As we shall see later Joe Scanlon had much the same ideas.

Management should undertake four main duties: (1) All the traditional knowledge which in the past may have been in the hands of the workmen should be gathered together and recorded, tabulated, perhaps even reduced to mathematical formulae. (2) There should be scientific selection and progressive development of workmen. (3) Science and scientifically selected and trained workmen should be brought together and (4) There should be almost equal division of actual work at the establishment between the workmen on the one hand and the management on the other. It is emphasized that scientific management is not philanthropic since no self-respecting workman wants to be given things; every man wants to earn them for himself. This evidence together with his other papers was reprinted in 1947.

Taylor's work has been described at some length because in one way or another it is the foundation from which by one route or another, the majority of management's attempts to motivate its workers have sprung even until the present time. It is fashionable now to belittle Taylor's activities and to decry his psychology. Taylor has often been blamed when there has been misapplication of his ideas which, it is alleged, have dehumanized the worker, and this especially by occupational psychologists because, so they say, Taylor did not know the psychological concepts of the 1960s. In particular his belief in the importance of money as a motivator is criticized on the grounds that surveys carried out in the 1950s suggest that it has a less important place in the hierarchy of items leading to job satisfaction than have other features of the work situation. These arguments would be a lot more convincing if a survey had been carried out in 1880, and it is surely stretching things a bit too far to say that because money may not be the most important thing to most people now, this was equally true eighty years ago.

In view of material from Taylor's writings which have been quoted above, it is a little difficult to go along with Blackler and Williams (1971) when they say that the modern view of the doctrine that money is *the* important factor in motivation was formulated by Taylor who was concerned to secure maximum output for minimum cost and whose solution was to regard men as individual machine-like units. 'While the social theory implicit in his work is bad enough (for example that men are essentially instruments manipulated by their employers) the pyschological assumptions are frightening.' A very different view is put forward by Drucker (1974): 'Taylor was the first man in the known history of mankind who did not take the work for granted, but looked at it and studied it ...' While Taylor in his approach to the worker was clearly a man of the nineteenth century, he started out with social rather than engineering or profit objectives. What led Taylor to his work and provided his motivation throughout was, first, a desire to free the worker from the burden of heavy toil, destructive of body and soul. And then it was the hope of breaking the 'Iron Law' of wages of the classical economists (including Marx) which condemned the worker to economic insecurity and to enduring poverty. Taylor's hope

– it has largely been fulfilled in the developed countries – was to make it possible to give the labourer a decent livelihood through increasing productivity of work.

Taylor himself seems to have adhered fairly closely to his own precepts. Others, however, taking the more convenient and profitable parts of his ideas, such as time study for instance, and being often untrained and inefficient in the practice of scientific management, caused a great deal of antagonism both among managements, the community and the workers. It is claimed that he became a hated man so far as the workers were concerned. There is no doubt that he has been made a scapegoat and has been misrepresented in many aspects of his ideas. For instance Blackler and Williams (1971) say 'He thought men were basically lazy, irrational and untrustworthy and that it was important that their energy should be channelled by exploiting their inherent greed ... it would seem from Taylor's assumptions that we need to distinguish an élite of self-controlled individuals whose role is to manipulate their fickle colleagues by astute use of the power of money!' This is really a little bit hard on Taylor.

Ernst Abbé and Zeiss

Although Taylor is the best known, he was not by any means the only industrialist to explore ways of motivating his employees. Of these, two examples will suffice. The first concerns Ernst Abbé who took over control of the Karl Zeiss works in Jena on Zeiss' death in 1888. Abbé was a university trained physicist and he set about systematically studying the operations carried out in the plant in the making of optical glass and then the conversion of optical glass into precision lenses. When he was satisfied that he had devised the best basic processes, he called together the master and journeymen from the plant, told them about his new techniques and methods and then asked *them* to organize the way the work was to be done and who was to do it. Thus the responsibility for organizing their work lay in the hands of the operatives themselves.

The new techniques obviously required new machinery and equipment and this too Abbé handed over to the skilled workers to develop with the assistance of appropriate engineers and scientists. Thus Abbé anticipated by three-quarters of a century the alleged innovations which have received so much publicity in the 1960s under the name *job enrichment*. Abbé's second innovation was the introduction of *continuous training* for his fully trained and highly skilled craftsmen by running courses which they were expected to attend at intervals throughout their working life. The object was not to train them so much for promotion, but to enable them to do their jobs more efficiently and to keep pace with the continuous improvements with which many of them were actively engaged. These highly skilled workers were expected to join with the scientists and engineers in a continuous effort to develop new products and new methods of work. There was no guarantee of employment at Zeiss but any man who was proficient and was prepared to work hard could be assured of his job even during less prosperous times. The philosophy was that a firm could not afford to carry passengers since this mitigated against the prosperity of the remainder of the workforce.

Thomas Watson and IBM

The second example is that of Thomas J. Watson Sr who founded International Business Machines (IBM) and was for many years its President. Unlike Taylor and Abbé, Watson doesn't seem to have set out deliberately to develop improved working methods; according to the story which is told he stumbled on the innovations more or less by chance when he found one of the workers waiting for a tool setter to alter the machine. Watson therefore introduced training schemes to enable the operatives to do their own tool setting and shortly afterwards, again with additional training, the inspection function was also given to the operative. This is what has now come to be called *job enlargement*. The improvements in output and quality were so unexpectedly large that IBM decided to apply the principle as widely as possible. To enable this to be done even with semi-skilled labour the various operations were made as simple as possible, but each worker was trained to do as many of the operations as was practicable. Not only was there an important increase in productivity, but also there was a change in the attitudes of the workers who took a particular pride in their jobs.

The second innovation at IBM was also serendipity and does not strictly belong to the period which we are discussing. Delays in the design of a piece of equipment required that the production started before the design was completed. The final details were therefore worked out with the engineers collaborating with the operatives on the shop floor. The result was that each operative, having taken part in engineering the product and determining his part in its construction, did a very much better and more productive job. It is now commonplace in IBM for the operative to get involved in the planning of the product, of the method of production and of his own job.

IBM's third innovation was to do away with the traditional pay incentives. In 1936 each worker was put on a straight salary and, instead of output norms being imposed from above, each worker developed his own rate of production in consultation with his foreman. Where work was familiar this was not at all difficult, but even when a new operation or major changes took place the establishment of the operative's production targets was left to the men themselves so that each could work out the speed and flow of work which would give him, as an individual, the greatest production. In addition to this each worker had his employment guaranteed even during the depression years of the thirties. Thus at a time when most other employers were using the fear of losing the job as an important motivator, IBM without this coercion was able to keep individual worker output improving whereas in most other industries it was declining in spite of high wage incentives.

There is one characteristic which is common to all the three individuals we have been discussing; they were all authoritarian, in fact Watson could be considered to be a tyrant. They demanded first-class performance and were not prepared to take good intentions as a substitute. None was at all reluctant to make decisions and to ensure that these decisions were carried out. Although this is not true of Taylor, Abbé and Watson, authoritarians though they were, were not particularly interested in organizing hierarchical authority. Just as they felt themselves to be *responsible* for making decisions at the level at which they were functioning, they equally felt that everyone else should take similar responsibility, and the lower down the hierarchy this responsibility could be devolved the better. So in a sense, everyone in the organization who was capable of doing so, could and was expected to exercise his authority where appropriate. This is the direct antithesis of the permissiveness of current ideas such as 'democratic management' or 'participatory democracy' which are primarily concerned with the organization of authority rather than responsibility.

Gain sharing plans

Henry Towne

Apart from the comparatively rare instances, of which examples have been quoted, of employers genuinely trying to motivate their workers by organizational changes, industry's efforts at motivation have been almost exclusively concentrated on the development of better and better wage incentive plans. So many of these were developed that their name is legion and the majority have disappeared almost without trace. A few, either because they introduced some fundamental new principle or because they were accompanied by competent publicity, have survived and are still discussed in textbooks on management, and some may even still be used today. The first of these innovators whom we may notice was Henry Towne of the Yale and Towne manufacturing company. Although he was an ardent supporter of Taylor, Towne's 'Gain Sharing Plan' was not derived from Taylor's ideas but was a form of yearly profit sharing. In 1886 he introduced a scheme to use his costing system as a 'basis for allotting to employees in a business a share of the gain or benefit accruing from their own efforts ... if at the end of the year the credit exceed the charges, I will divide the resulting gain, or reduction in cost with you, retaining to myself one portion, say a half and distributing the other portion amongst you pro rata on the basis of wages earned by each during the year.' The present author worked under just such a scheme in a Bristol printing firm in the late thirties and while it was very nice to have a substantial handout once a year, it was too far removed from individual efforts for it to be much of a motivator.

Frederick Halsey
The plan was modified by Frederick Halsey of the Rand Drill Company who applied Towne's ideas on a daily or weekly basis. As time study had not yet extended beyond Taylor's companies, Halsey's method was to establish a normal production from the record of performances in previous months and then to pay a premium for the production in excess of this norm. If the norm was not achieved, workers were paid so much per hour for the amount of time worked which effectively guaranteed a minimum daily wage. The important departure here was from the general principle of piece-work which gave no such guarantee. When more accurate methods of measurement became available, they started dividing the savings which may have accrued as a result of extra effort in a proportion, usually 50:50, between the operatives and the management (with sometimes a proportion to the immediate supervision). After 1898 this method spread very rapidly first under the name of the Towne–Halsey plan and in more recent years known simply as the Halsey plan.

The Gantt plan

One of Taylor's associates at the Bethlehem Steel Works was Henry Gantt (1861–1919) who not only followed Taylor's principles in almost every respect but seems to have been far more successful than him in his relationship with employees. In 1901 he developed what he called a task and bonus plan. He believed that operatives would be just as well motivated if he replaced Taylor's punitive piece-rate, when operatives didn't meet the norm, with a low time guarantee so that in effect there was day rate up to the norm and piece-work above it. There is nothing particularly revolutionary in this; Gantt's important contribution was that he realized that whether or not an operative achieved the norm depended to a large extent on whether *management* had the work properly organized so that everything that was required would be available in the right place at the right time and of the right quality. He devised progress charts to be used for planning and control but he also devised a man-record chart which showed visually for all to see how well each individual was performing.

It is worth recounting a personal experience of the importance of the operatives' efforts being backed by good management control. A new assembly line had been installed by the Ergonomics Department of TI (Group Services) Limited in a manufacturing company in Birmingham. The new line had been mocked-up in the Ergonomics Department and so a fairly close relationship had been established between people working on the project and the girls who were going to work the line. From performance on the mock-up output was estimated and indicated that management would have to take a number of actions, such as ordering additional material, increasing the output of the plating shop and, in particular, strengthening the quality control in the machine shop. In spite of repeated prodding, no action was taken.

When the line was started up everything went splendidly; the girls wanted to show what they could do and all expectations were realized. But then the trouble started; parts that should have gone together easily had to be forced so that the smooth flow of the line was interrupted. Then shortages of parts developed so that every so often the line had to stop for lack of components and the girls had to sit around, sometimes for hours at a time, with nothing to do except to sing rather pointedly the old songs *Why are we waiting* and *We are all browned off*. Eventually, everything was sorted out and the line ran smoothly. But it never again achieved more than about two-thirds the production which had been achieved at the outset. The girls gave their reasons for this quite openly in the form 'we made a real effort but management didn't back us up, so why the hell should we bother now?' As they were on straight piece-work they were able to bargain a price which gave them an adequate wage without their having to increase their production to that which they could have achieved.

We have already mentioned that the very low rate paid under the Taylor plan when production was below the norm was punitive and greatly disliked by the workers. It was this relatively small part of Taylor's philosophy which caused him to be so reviled, particularly by the labour unions. Another of his colleagues, D. V. Merrick, devised an alternative plan (similar in some way to Gantt's plan) in which Taylor's 'one big step' was divided into two. So at about 83 per cent of the norm half the difference in some versions, 40 per cent in others is added to the piece-rate, the remainder being added when production reaches the norm. Merrick claimed that his plan of giving rewards earlier was a great encouragement to new operatives who had not yet acquired sufficient skill to reach the norm.

Bedaux point premium plan

It was an era of experiment and innovation. There were a great many other named plans; most of these are now forgotten and their names only occur in books giving an overview and comparison of incentive plans, e.g. Lytle (1942). One of these was the Emmerson plan which is only worth mentioning now because of the part it played in the development of the Bedaux plan. Round about 1913 A. M. Morrini went from France to the United States to investigate scientific management. When he returned he took with him three Emmerson and two Taylor engineers. Charles Bedaux (an émigré Frenchman) went with the party as interpreter. When war was declared Bedaux joined the French Foreign Legion but somehow or other managed to return to the United States by 1916. In the course of his duties as an interpreter he had become familiar with the Emmerson techniques and he started installing them in several companies in about 1919. But he really wanted something of his own and, being a born salesman, he was able to develop some new ideas which have had a profound effect even until now (Bedaux, 1921). His basic concept was quite simple. He invented a new unit which he called a 'Bedaux' or 'B' for short which was a unit of work per minute together with a proper allowance for fatigue. This unit was established on the basis that someone working at a day-rate pace could produce sixty Bs per hour and this was established as a norm and was paid for at a rate equivalent to day-rate. However, a well motivated operative should be able to do eighty Bs in an hour and an operative achieving this level would be paid a bonus at, usually, 75 per cent of the base rate per unit. Instead of, as in piece-work, a price per piece being established, a value in Bs or decimal parts of Bs was given to each part. As, at the norm, a B is equal to one minute, this was equivalent to giving time rates in minutes and decimal minutes which is the current practice. The B values were all established by time study and Bedaux realized that time study was useless without an estimate of the rate (in terms of Bs) and the effort which was being put into the work. By introducing this rating procedure he was able to normalize time studies down to his standard of 60 Bs.

Rating has been under fire ever since, particularly since World War Two, on the grounds that at slow speeds there was a tendency to overrate and at high work speeds there is a tendency to underrate. On these grounds it is claimed that human subjective judgement is too inaccurate to have any validity. Bedaux was not a psychologist, nor for that matter was he an engineer, and most of the people using the rating technique were not psychologists either, so it was not until very recently that it was pointed out (Murrell, 1974) that rating, like every other subjective judgement, will be logarithmic. Most psychologists have tended recently to decry the Bedaux system and all that has developed from it, partly on the grounds that it concerns industry and money and is therefore 'unacademic' and not worthy of serious consideration, and partly because there has been a 'view' that financial incentives are relatively unimportant compared with non-financial ones about which many books have been written. So rating has been allowed to continue for more than fifty years without anyone suggesting, until 1974, the application of Fechner's or Steven's laws (see A5). As it is a situation has developed in which current schemes for paying bonuses are acting as serious brakes upon production (Murrell, 1971). It was this rating which caused the greatest opposition from the unions to the Bedaux plan.

As it was, Bedaux introduced three important innovations: an allowance for fatigue; the practice of rating speed and effort which the operatives put into the task; and the use of time-related units rather than money as the 'price' for each piece of work. It is worth mentioning, although it is not really relevant to our subject, that this innovation enabled Bedaux to develop a whole system of production control based on his B units which has formed the basis from which the modern techniques of work study have sprung.

We have seen that in the last quarter of the nineteenth century and the first quarter of the twentieth century a whole series of payment systems were developed with the idea of motivating the employees by financial incentives. Very little has changed since. At the same time and alongside the financial incentives, a whole series of other approaches, which would probably now be called non-financial incentives, were tried. Those anticipated, often by more than half a century, more recent developments by social scientists, including psychologists, such as 'job enlargement', 'job enrichment' and 'worker participation'. It is interesting to note that many of the books written in the last fifteen or twenty years and particularly those which have emanated from the management schools all contain references, sometimes extensive, to the work of Taylor and some of the other names which have been discussed above.

Motion study

While it is clear that financial incentives were intended to motivate operatives to produce more it is not so easy to see a direct connection with the motion study which Frank and Lillian Gilbreth developed in the late 1880s. The professed objective of motion study was the elimination of unnecessary movement and the tidy organization of the work place with the idea of increasing output. That improved output might lead to increased earnings might be expected, but this was hardly ever the case because as soon as a new method was devised, new rates were established so that earnings would remain static while ouput was increased. What Gilbreth did claim was that his methods led to a reduction of fatigue, a greater feeling of well-being, and the removal of the frustrations associated with disorganized work places. In more recent times the installation of financial incentives has almost invariably been accompanied by changes of method so it is virtually impossible to disentangle the effect of one or the other as a cause of increased output. But taken together, as they usually were under the title 'time and motion study' and now re-named 'work study', most managements considered their practice as motivators. Incidentally, Lillian Gilbreth was a psychologist as also is Anne Shaw who did so much to develop the practice of motion study (or method study as it later came to be called) since 1939. Although it is now still practised as part of work study by some managements, method study on the whole tended to be superseded by ergonomics in its capacity of fitting the whole of the job to the man, not just the movements which he makes.

The Scanlon plan

The idea that management and the workers should collaborate in improving productivity is not a new one. As we have seen, it was one of the basic tenets of Taylor's scientific management. But as so often happens, it takes someone with the right personality who is at the right time and at the right place to suddenly give the impetus which brings an idea to wide acceptance. By all accounts Joe Scanlon was a remarkable man. In 1936 he was working in a small firm in Ohio called Adamson. At that time the steel workers were being organized and Scanlon became the president of the new local branch. At the beginning of 1938 the steel company was heading for bankruptcy and Scanlon and his fellow union officers persuaded the president of the company to go to Pittsburgh to see Clinton Golden, then vice-president of the Steel Workers' Union. They put the case to him; the company was virtually on the rocks and the union was demanding higher wages, the only effect of which would be to sink the company without trace. Golden (1958) describes his astonishment at the arrival of this deputation and tells of the advice which he gave. 'I suggested that the group return to the mill and arrange to interview every employee in an effort to enlist his aid and familiarity with work processes in eliminating waste, improving efficiency, reducing cost and improving the quality of the products in order to keep assured of the survival of the company.'

His advice was accepted and under Scanlon's leadership and with the full cooperation of the management, they set about a pioneering effort in management–union cooperation. As a result costs were reduced and the quality of the product improved, the company was able to grant wage increases and on top of that the men received a bonus. And this was the period when other companies were going to the wall.

Although all this cooperation was developed with the idea of survival it laid the foundations of what became known as the Scanlon plan. There were so many companies in the late thirties that were getting into difficulties that Scanlon was persuaded to move into the national headquarters of the Steel Workers' Union and to apply his ideas more widely. As a result, they were installed in between forty and fifty companies.

Douglas McGregor (who developed Theory X and Theory Y which will be discussed below) got to hear about Scanlon's activities and persuaded him to move in 1942 to MIT where he remained until he died in 1956.

The Scanlon plan is different from most of the other productivity 'plans' in that it is not a formula for the distribution of bonuses or profits. McGregor describes it as a way of industrial life – a philosophy of management. It consists basically of two parts. The first is a device for sharing any economic gains which may accrue from improvements in productivity – a unique kind of cost-reduction sharing. It does not replace the normal, competitive salary and wage structure, but is superimposed on it. The method for determining cost-reduction uses a ratio between the total man-power costs and a measure of output such as the total sales or the value added. The second feature involves a formal method of providing each individual in the firm with an opportunity to contribute his brains and ingenuity to the improvement of productivity. It differed from the normal idea of the suggestion box, which is so often abused, in that everyone had a chance either informally or formally of putting forward ideas, participating in evaluating them and being encouraged to develop them to their maximum. The important characteristic of the Scanlon suggestion scheme is that it is collective, there is no individual pay off, each individual is expected to contribute his ideas for the benefit of everyone else. In the literature there are a number of examples of the success which followed from the introduction of a Scanlon plan for which there was quite a vogue in the early 1950s. Very little is said or written now about Scanlon plans and the extent to which these have continued to operate in the companies in which they were installed is not at all clear.

At about the same time a very similar plan was developed in the United Kingdom by Russon and after the war in the United States by Rucker, whose scheme was based on a 'production value' which was derived by deducting the cost of incoming materials and supplies from the value of the sales. By studying data available between the years 1899 and 1954 Rucker found that the hourly-paid workers received very consistently about 40 per cent of this production value. This alternative which does not seem to have included all the characteristics of the Scanlon plan was said to have been adopted by more than forty British companies by 1958.

By joint consultation is meant the setting up of machinery by which management and workers (organized or unorganized) will meet at regular intervals to discuss common problems in the conduct of their enterprise. It does not cover the allocation of greater responsibility to individuals in the work-force and discussion with them on the exercise of these responsibilities. Examples of joint consultation before 1939 are comparatively rare, but there are one or two instances, notably the Harwood Manufacturing Company where the initial moves were made just before the outbreak of war but where the outcome was not reported until somewhat later. These have therefore been included as post-1939.

Just after the end of the First World War there was an effort made jointly by business men and politicians to introduce consultation into British industry. The Liberal Party organized a series of conferences and produced a detailed volume outlining plans for collaboration in industry. A Bill requiring the setting up of joint industrial councils in all major industries was introduced into the Commons in 1922 by Frank Murrell, a Cardiff master printer; although the Bill received its second reading it never became law because of the fall of the government and the subsequent general election. The only relics of this effort are the Whitley Councils which operate in some of the Civil Service Departments; in their activities they fall far short of the ideals of those who were working for closer collaboration in industry in those early days.

Whether the Joint Industrial Council Bill would have achieved much if it had become law is open to some doubt, since the general attitude of employers at that time was that the worker's place was on the shop floor where he did what he was told and if he didn't like doing it he could always go somewhere else.

But there were enlightened employers, amongst whom the Quakers were prominent. Seebohm Rowntree established a Central Works Council at the Cocoa Works in York just after the First World War, and he made a practice of discussing all important decisions with the Council. In 1921 Rowntree decided that a trained psychologist should be put on to the staff of Rowntrees (Higham, 1955). Since joint consultation on a formal basis had been set up the proposal to appoint a psychologist was referred to the Central Works Council, where it was greeted with scepticism and even hostile criticism. Eventually a Joint Management–Council committee was set up and after due deliberation it recommended to the Central Works Council that the appointment should be agreed and that the type of work the psychologist would do should be defined and approved by the Works Council. As a result psychologists have been employed at Rowntrees until now, mainly on personnel work, including placement in the right kind of jobs (see E2). A case is mentioned where a group of inefficient workers was given notice and the psychology department, having tested them, placed them in other jobs where they became efficient (memories of Taylor and his 'first-class men').

The Human Relations Movement of Elton Mayo had in it the germs of joint consultation but its protagonists were much more concerned with explaining how people related to each other than in setting up formal machinery to enable them to react. They were far too busy concentrating on the relationship between individuals working together so that the work which the people were doing and the conditions under which they did it and the rewards which they received did not merit any attention. Nevertheless, the sudden interest in joint consultation immediately after World War Two had some of its roots in human relations, because practical individuals who may never have heard of Mayo were taking the term human relations to mean that both sides of industry must get closer together.

Other work

Very few actual experiments (that is, observation of the effect of controlled changes as distinct from making observations and recording opinions) appear to have been carried out prior to 1939, other than the Hawthorne studies and research by the IHRB and NIIP. One of the very few experiments which has been reported (Feldman, 1937) was into the relationship between supervision and output. In 1933 group incentives were introduced into twenty-two sections, covering about 1,000 employees, in an insurance company. The bonus was paid on the basis of cost-saving of each group over the costs of the previous twelve months. This bonus was over and above the normal salaries and was paid to all in the group including the supervisor. In the first year all sections showed an improvement but some showed a greater improvement than others, the range being from 2 to 12 per cent.

In 1934 the management shifted the section heads so that those who had been in charge of above-average sections now took over sections which had been below-average and vice versa. The main reason for doing this was to find out whether differences in the results were due to the supervision, or to the supervised, or to the working conditions. The results for the second year showed further increases in all sections ranging now from 6 to 18 per cent. The supervisors who had done well in the first year also did well in the second year, even though they were now supervising groups who had done badly in the first year. Finally, in 1935 the supervisors were reassigned to sections on a chance basis, and they maintained their same ranks as they had in the two preceding years.

The fact that performance improved when the change was made might be taken as evidence of the importance of the desire for money. But clearly there is far more to it than that as some supervisors seemed better able than others to motivate members of their groups to achieve a high level of performance. It does not appear from Feldman's account that any attempt was made to explain what it was about the different supervisors which produced this result.

Apart from these experimental studies some industrial psychologists, sociologists and management theorists became increasingly interested in the industrial scene. The techniques they used were mainly aimed at assessing employee morale, job satisfaction and other attitudes to employment by the development of opinion surveys, and to some extent by the

43

use of the direct observation of behaviour. They became particularly concerned with the activities of management in its attempts to motivate its employees in such a way that the various payment schemes, the techniques of time study were investigated and commented upon, e.g. Uhrbrock (1935). A start was made in the study of group behaviour and in particular restriction of output which was becoming such an important factor in industrial efficiency. Many industrialists seem to have been aware of what was going on and to have accepted restriction of output as just another difficult factor to be coped with. So, although it is very frequently mentioned, very few attempts seem to have been made in the pre-1939 period. The unions as they gained in strength and organizing power stated quite openly that they were controlling output with the purpose of increasing their power, and during the slump to spread out available work and to avoid lay-offs (Lytle, 1938). Restrictions might take the form of specifying the number of bricks a bricklayer could lay in a day (Watkins, 1929), or by specifying the maximum amount of money which an operative could earn by piece-work or bonus when the product varied. If an operative produced more than was permitted, they would 'bank' it and this did not by any means always involve the physical holding back of the work. But it was known that some employees had built up such a 'hump' that if they hadn't had to come in to fill in their daily time sheets they could have taken a holiday for six months.

An interesting and detailed study is that of Mathewson (1931) who surveyed opinion to some extent but obtained his main information by the technique of direct observation, i.e. by taking a job himself as a labourer, as a machine operator and other jobs, and living in the communities. In addition Mathewson was able to recruit six workers who reported to him regularly. The main fact which emerged was that output was restricted primarily because of fear that the rates would be cut if it went up. The group exercised quite a strong influence over its members and used any means available to it to ensure that the norms were not exceeded. Another but less important objective seems to have been to protect the less competent or the older workers.

This technique of participative observation was all too rarely used. There is another example from an even earlier period when Williams, personnel director of a company, got a job on the railways, in the mines and in factories both in America and in Europe. His experiences were summarized in three books, the last of which was published in 1925. At that time group determination of the financial rewards does not seem to have been so prevalent as it became later. Williams reported that the main driving force in the people with whom he came into contact was the desire for money, with the desire for status as a close second from amongst a number of others. In view of this restrictiveness, which was known to most people associated with industry, the great discovery of Hawthorne that groups of men organized themselves to restrict output and to resist change (see p. 64) was, as Landsberger (1958) points out, very much of an anti-climax.

The alternative to the use of participative observation was to carry out surveys of workers' attitudes. The massive survey undertaken by the Western Electric Company was part of the Hawthorne studies, but apart from this the number of other investigations carried out was miniscule compared with the post-1939 flood. Articles appeared in journals from time to time (e.g. Kornhauser and Sharp, 1932, which was basically a study of the effects of poor supervision) or books (e.g. Hoppock, 1935). There is no evidence that any of this work, such as it was, had any impact at all on industry which still persisted in believing that financial rewards were the only motivators to higher performance.

Most of the work which has been described, in so far as it was undertaken by psychologists, would have been undertaken by people who would consider themselves to be industrial psychologists and they were publishing books under that title, for example Viteles (1932), or Myers (1926).

The importance of the group in determining industrial behaviour requires that the behaviour of the individuals within the group should also be studied, and this should involve social psychology which had emerged much earlier than industrial psychology as a separate area of study, for example, Ross (1908). Its importance lay in asking why an individual would act differently when he was a member of a group than he would do when he was on his own and why he might behave differently in one group or in another. The problems of motivation in industry are primarily problems of social interaction of the kind described. It is indeed odd that so little research can be identified as clearly belonging to social psychologists. It was early sociologists who developed an interest in the industrial field, such as Thomas (1904) and Cooley (1909), and it is sociologists who have, so it would seem, been the people principally concerned with the study of the social aspects of industrial activity in the pre-1939 period.

3
Research associated activities – pre-1939

In this chapter we shall look at the industrial investigations carried out by people who are not employed in industry. We shall also look at an extensive research programme carried out by management in its own plant but with considerable assistance from some academics.

Industrial Fatigue Research Board

The circumstances which led to the setting up of the Industrial Fatigue Research Board towards the end of World War One are described in some detail in E4. The Health of Munition Workers' Committee from which the IFRB developed was set up because the imposition of very long working hours resulted in a decrease rather than the expected increase in production, in greater absenteeism and greater sickness. For anyone who has read so far the mention of the length of working hours and its effect on rate of production will ring a bell; one of Taylor's experiments in this field was briefly reported in the preceding chapter. Taylor was not the only person before World War One who had been experimenting with rest pauses and shorter working hours and who had shown that rate of production decreased when hours of work increased. It seems curious therefore that a decision should have been taken to extend the already long working hours to ten, twelve or even sixteen hours per day (Vernon, 1921). However, it seems unlikely that a country solicitor like Lloyd George (who was then Minister of Munitions), or the career civil servants who advised him, had ever heard of Taylor's research (if they had even heard of Taylor at all). In the event, it may have been just as well they had not, because if they had behaved sensibly it might well be that we would never have had the Industrial Fatigue Research Board nor, possibly, even the National Institute of Industrial Psychology and we should have been very much the poorer without the wealth of knowledge on the natural history of industry which they produced.

The Board's investigators carried out a very wide range of investigations including straightforward motion studies, which is a little odd when one remembers that they were supported by the Medical Research Council (MRC). The studies which are most relevant to our interest are those on financial incentives, work/rest schedules, pacing by machine, monotony and boredom, and 'music while you work'. Useful results in any of these areas could, to use a modern phrase, improve the quality of the working life and then, it seems implicitly to be assumed, you have achieved some form of non-financial incentive. Many of the things which the Board did (it changed its name in 1928 to the Industrial Health Research Board) achieved increases, sometimes substantial, in production. Many of their research findings have now become recognized practices in a number of industries. The introduction of 'music while you work' in the form in which it was used during World War Two was a direct consequence of the report of Wyatt and Langdon (1937) who conducted a twenty-four-week study of the effects of gramophone music as a part of a larger study of boredom. There is nothing particularly new in the use of music in factories, but what Wyatt and Langdon did was to establish that there were particular schedules which appeared to be superior in improving output to others, and it was these schedules which were adopted for 'music while you work' shortly after the outbreak of the war.

The IHRB was also increasingly interested in selection and training, particularly in the thirties. Here again the work seems to be based on the implicit belief that an individual will wish to work harder and better if he has been selected for a job which matches his capacities and is properly trained to do it.

Incentives in repetitive work – an IHRB investigation

Right from the outset the Industrial Fatigue/Health Research Board had interested itself in factors of the work situation which might be regarded as motivators. Its first two reports published in 1919 were about hours of work, and its investigators moved on to look at various aspects of repetitive work including rest pauses, variety and uniformity. The series ended in 1937 with a study of monotony and boredom. The work of the Board's investigators ranged over a much wider area than this but the research which has been mentioned is the main work which is relevant to the subject of this book.

The report which will be described in some detail was published in 1934, was undertaken by Sam Wyatt with the assistance of L. Frost and F. G. L. Stock and was called *Incentives in Repetitive Work: a practical experiment in a factory*.

The experiment was concerned with behaviour of operatives as individuals during the learning period using the technique of controlled experiment in an industrial environment. Ten girls aged between 15 and 16 years were recruited with the use of various selection tests for the experiment which lasted for 54 weeks. The factory was one which made confectionery and five operations were studied: (i) unwrapping pieces of toffee which had been imperfectly wrapped (ii) wrapping chocolates in foil (iii) packing squares of wrapped toffee in tins, closing and fixing the lid (iv) weighing a filled tin with wrapped pieces of toffee and fitting a lid (v) weighing out 4 lbs of wrapped toffee, putting it into a large tin lined with decorative paper, putting on the lid, wrapping in brown paper and tying with string. These jobs increased in variety and complexity from 1 to 5 and the number of units of output which would be produced in the same time were respectively 40, 20, 12, 6 and 1. Unlike the normal factory practice each girl learned all the operations. Two girls at a time were assigned to each operation and they rotated the job in a 5 × 5 Latin square design (see A8) on different days of the week. (Essentially this means that each girl had a turn at each job.) Three different methods of payment were used. A fixed weekly wage for the first nine weeks, a competitive bonus system for the next fifteen weeks and a straight piece-rate for another twelve weeks. Over a period of thirty-six weeks these were the only changes which were made.

A word must be said about the competitive bonus system. The normal alternative to day-rate during training was piecework, but this was not often used, either because the earnings at the outset would be too low or, to avoid this, the prices would have to be progressively changed and this was considered to be undesirable. The competitive bonus system was devised and tested as a possible alternative. Each week the girls were ranked according to their output and the slowest worker got her normal wage. The next slowest was given an additional sixpence and so on up the ranking so that the fastest worker received an extra four shillings and six pence. Unfortunately, we are not told what the basic rate of pay was, but it seems probable it was in the region of seven shillings and six pence or ten shillings. The extra that could be earned was substantial.

The girls worked for eight hours a day split evenly into two four-hour periods, with one hour break in the middle.

The results are presented in two ways. First, output was averaged per week overall and, secondly, it was presented for each individual job; in both cases it is given as a percentage of the output in the first week.

Over the first nine weeks, and as learning took place, there was an improvement of about 12½ per cent but this was mainly due to two jobs of 'wrapping' and 'weighing and wrapping'. The other three jobs, particularly the 'unwrapping', tended to go down throughout the period. At this point the bonus rate was introduced and there was an immediate jump of a further 46 to 58 per cent above base. It would appear that the jump was much the same for all five tasks. This system of payment lasted for twelve weeks during which there was a further 20 per cent increase in relative output, but once again there was a marked difference between the different jobs with 'wrapping and weighing' and 'wrapping' contributing most of the increase, 'packing' remaining relatively static, 'weighing' declining somewhat, and 'unwrapping' dropping quite markedly. Piece-rate was then introduced and production again shot up from 78 to 122 per cent above base. Once again all the tasks contributed to this improvement which remained fairly static at about this level for the remainder of the experiment which lasted twelve weeks. This time there was relatively little difference in trend between the five jobs, none showing any greater improvement than any other. It must be remembered that in any one week all the girls contributed to the production score.

At this point a new experiment was started. All three methods of payment were tested simultaneously for a period of six weeks. It is not stated whether the girls continued to rotate in their Latin square design but it seems that this is likely. The 'wrapping' and 'packing' jobs remained on piece-work and showed very little change, 'weighing' and 'weighing and wrapping' were put on bonus, the first showing an increase of nearly 10 per cent and the latter of nearly 15 per cent. 'Unwrapping' was put on time-work and showed a decrease of 25 per cent. Too much should not be read into this particular experiment, since a change from bonus to piece-work had produced a substantial increase, and then a change back to bonus introduced a further increase which could not possibly have been due to the effects of practice. Although the 'unwrapping' went down on time-work it did not descend to anywhere near its original level. Although these results are explained by the experimenters, their explanations lack conviction.

The job was then changed and all the girls were put on to filling small cartons with tablets. Half of them appear to have been paid on the bonus scheme and the other half on day-rate. This was in order to demonstrate the suitability of the competitive bonus scheme in the learning situation. After nine weeks the relative output on bonus was about 35 per cent above that for time-rate and was continuing to rise. To confirm these results three further experiments were carried out. In the first, a group of 19 girls who were engaged on the same job of packing tablets as the original experimental group; ten of these were paid day-rate throughout but the remaining nine were put on to piece-work after the first five days. The output of both groups was identical over the first five days but thereafter the groups diverge, and after thirty days the piece-work group was producing about 25 per cent more than the time-rate group. In the second experiment a group of girls who were employed on feeding machines with toffee worked for eight days on a day-rate but were offered a bonus when the daily output exceeding 60,000 pieces. There was an immediate sharp increase from about 50,000 to 60,000, at which point the production remained static until the twenty-fourth day when the output target was raised to 68,000 pieces; there was again an immediate jump which was maintained until the end of the experiment after thirty-eight days.

The final experiment involved an unspecified number of experienced girls who were employed in feeding wrapping machines with chocolate. Their hourly output was recorded over a period of twenty-seven weeks on time-rate; piece-rate was then introduced for a further twenty-six weeks. The introduction of piece-work caused an improvement in production of about one-third, but what was also noticeable was that stoppages were both shorter and less frequent.

The original experiment is analysed in a good deal of detail giving individual results and comparisons, variations in output during the working day, analysis of lost time. Changes in the behaviour of the girls is worth comment. On day-rate, conduct which disturbed or distracted the other girls was comparatively frequent but there were very few quarrels and complaints; on the bonus and piece-work these disturbances went down but the quarrels were highest under bonus while the complaints were highest under piece-work. Since the bonus scheme was a competitive one it is not perhaps surprising that the personal rivalry which the system must have engendered did cause a good deal of quarrelling; quarrelling was less under piece-work but it was still substantially more than when on day-rate. It was noted that generally the girls with the worst performance caused the most trouble. Other aspects of which details are given include the study of the girls' preferences, an analysis of lost time, a study of group and individual differences, the effects of rearranging workers within the group by changing the pairing, and a good deal of comment on the personality and behaviour of the individuals. In fact it is very difficult to think of anything else which might have been included in the investigation.

The experimenters felt that they had demonstrated quite clearly the superiority of payment-by-results over day-rate, but the major part of their discussion is about the behaviour of the girls independently and collectively. This discussion is factual and avoids all high falutin' theorizing about the deeper social meanings underlying the behaviour. In this it contrasts very markedly with the treatment of the results of the Hawthorne experiment which are about to be described.

The experimental design didn't allow a clear differentiation between the two wage incentive schemes, since the increases reported may have been related to some extent to the order in which they were administered. It appears that the girls themselves regarded piece-work as the fairest method of payment because individual earnings were dependent upon individual effort, whereas in the bonus system it depended on producing better results than the other girls. There was certainly less quarrelling and other troublesome conduct under piece-work which also tended to produce closer application to the work with less talking and a reduction of frequency and duration of stoppages.

The National Institute of Industrial Psychology

The NIIP, whose history is also mentioned in E4, worked very closely with the IFRB and a number of its reports cover the same ground. Like the IHRB, the NIIP moved increasingly into selection and training; the remnants of the IHRB were disbanded in 1967 and the NIIP ceased trading in 1973.

The tendency to move away from the collection of data on the shop floor which began to be apparent in the thirties continued after the war until the end, and over this period it is difficult to find more than a very few papers in the lists of those which have been published which seems to have involved the investigator actually getting down on to the shop floor and observing and recording what is going on. It is difficult to assess after the passage of so much time just how much effect investigations of these two groups of researchers had upon industrial practice. The IHRB was paid for by central funds but the NIIP depended upon the extent to which industrial and commercial firms were willing to meet the cost of an investigation by institute staff into conditions in their establishments. Since industry was paying for investigations to be carried out, it would be surprising if they did not use the information for which they had paid and the early reports give quite detailed accounts of the changes, including the design of work places, which were made. The investigators were clearly aware that they could improve *job satisfaction*, though whether the industrialists who were paying fees for the work thought of anything other than increasing *output* is open to doubt.

The situation with the work of the IHRB was rather different in that it was not being paid for by individual industrialists, and although detailed and extensive reports were published of each investigation it is not known exactly what impact these had. Labour was at that time still an expendable commodity and industrialists on the whole had to have a reason for bothering their heads about it. It was there, available in quantity, and it was always possible to replace anyone who was dissatisfied with the conditions of work. One or two did recognize that such hidden costs as labour turnover could arise from poor adjustment of people to their working life and to lack of motivation; but these were very few and far between. So industry was not avidly looking for new panaceas, as was to happen in the post-war period. The IHRB reports were widely available and members of the staff of the NIIP wrote some books such as *Industrial Psychology in Great Britain* by Charles Myers in 1926; Myers also edited *Industrial Psychology*, first published in 1929, which was reprinted no less than seven times. In 1932 G. H. Miles wrote the *Problems of Incentives in Industry* and co-authored with H. J. Welsh *Industrial Psychology in Practice* in the same year. Even so, industrial practice in the 1930s showed relatively little evidence that the ideas emanating from these researchers were having very much impact.

The Hawthorne studies

It is difficult to place the Hawthorne studies in the classification which has been adopted in this book because they were undoubtedly a research activity although they were sponsored by management. The management did not act on its own, it had the assistance of academics such as Elton Mayo and F. J. Roethlisberger, while much of the data was analysed by T. N. Whitehead. All three were at the Harvard School of Business Administration. This being so, it is a little difficult to understand why the experiments showed so many faults in design and why the effects of the faults on the results went unrecognized or, if they were recognized, were glossed over. To be charitable, though, we must remember that techniques of experimentation (particularly experimentation on the shop floor) were nothing like so well-developed then as now. It is nevertheless very difficult indeed to understand how anyone with even a grain of scientific training could ignore the effects of the substitution of two poor subjects by two good ones about one-third of the way through the experiment.

When most people hear the word 'Hawthorne', they immediately think of the 'Hawthorne effect' without having the foggiest idea who, what or where Hawthorne was. The general proposition of the so-called Hawthorne effect is that if you make any change in working conditions, it is the very fact that you have interested yourself in a group of operatives which makes them improve their performance, not the actual change itself; it is a social rather than a physical effect. While it is true that this can happen under certain circumstances, it cannot, as we shall show, really be a valid conclusion from the Hawthorne experiments themselves. It all goes to show how a bit of bad experimentation, written so that important facts are obscured and some false conclusions drawn, can lead to the development of a bit of industrial folklore which was not justified by the results obtained. Just how many people who talk glibly about the 'Hawthorne effect' have ever actually scientifically studied the first-hand accounts of what happened? Precious few we suspect. Volumes have been written about the Hawthorne experiments and chapters have appeared in many books, particularly those concerned with industrial relations. Each author according to his interests finding something to support his own particular point of view. As one said 'never has so much been written about so little'. Be that as it may, the Hawthorne studies did provide an empirical and even ideological basis for the Human Relations School, of which Elton Mayo was the principal exponent, for more than a decade.

Before looking at what the Hawthorne experiments did or did not achieve, something must be said about the experiments themselves. They are named after the Western Electric Company's Hawthorne Works near Chicago. The research lasted from 1924 until 1932 when, due to the depression, the girls taking part were sacked. The whole thing started with an investigation into the effect of lighting levels on production in conjunction with the National Research Council of the National Academy of Sciences, the brief being to study 'the relation of quality and quantity of illumination to efficiency in industry'. This research lasted two and a half years and is a classical example of applying the techniques of the physical sciences to the solution of human problems. It very quickly became clear that the rise and fall of output bore no direct relationship to the levels of illumination.

Following this two groups were set up, a test group and a control group, which were even put into separate buildings so that there could be no reaction between the two. Unfortunately, both groups showed appreciable increases in productivity and differences between them were not statistically significant. Several other things were tried; for example two women were set to work in a locked room where the light was reduced until it was approximately equal to that of moonlight, yet they were still able to maintain their rate of production and they reported no effects of eye strain or fatigue. In another experiment the subjects were led to believe that there had been a change in the illumination level when the light bulbs were taken out and replaced by bulbs of the same wattage; the level of performance was unaffected. As a result of these experiments it became quite clear that the level of illumination was playing only a very small part in determining the level of productivity; the next series of experiments were instituted with the express purpose of attempting to discover what the additional factors involved might be.

In the planning and conduct of the second series of experiments a crucial part was played by Elton Mayo (1880–1949), an Australian-born psychologist, who worked for most of his life at the Harvard Business School. He was the main originator and protagonist of the Human Relations School.

As Mayo conceived it, human relations is the study of the relationships between people working together. What they were actually doing, that is the work itself, was considered to be virtually irrelevant and received almost no attention. The human relations approach also recognized the failure of the traditional method of communication from management to the shop floor. It enjoined listening so that instead of starting out with the ideas which management wanted to get across to the shop floor, they should try to find out what it is the shop floor wants to know, is interested in and is receptive to. These ideas were developed more than forty years ago in Mayo's book, *The Human Problems of an Industrial Civilization*, but nowadays his ideas have very little impact on industrial practice.

This then was the outlook of the academic who was most involved in the Hawthorne exercise, and it is not surprising that bias towards Mayo's ethos coloured the conclusions which were subsequently drawn from the work (Roethlisberger and Dickson, 1939). In launching on the experiments in what has become known as the relay assembly test room, the management had quite clear objectives in mind; these were to study fatigue and boredom and their effects upon production; the extent to which they could be ameliorated by giving rest pauses, shorter working days, change in the kind of equipment; and finally the attitudes of the workers towards their work and towards the company.

The assembly of magnetic relays was chosen as the task to be investigated. The normal output was in the region of 500 per day which was sufficiently large for fluctuations in output as a consequence of experimental changes to be reasonably easily observable. Six girls took part in the experiment, five of them assembling the relays and the sixth being a 'layout operator' who was in effect a service girl providing the materials for the assemblers and taking away and sorting the finished relays. The work was batch-work, i.e. the nature of the relays changed at regular intervals. In spite of efforts to reduce the variety as much as possible, up to forty different types of relay were assembled during the early periods of the experiment. Unfortunately, it does not always take the same time to assemble each type of relay, so from the outset the experimenters had introduced a variable into their experiments over which they had no control. They did however work on the theory that if the experimental periods went on long enough the 'mix' would be much the same in each period, and so the effect of assembling different relays would cancel itself out. Later on in the experiment they did manage substantially to reduce the variety of relays being assembled, and this in itself must have affected the comparability of the early and late periods. The only other person in the room was the observer who was conducting the experiment, who was there instead of a fore-woman. This introduced 'friendly supervision' and social factors which were claimed to be the predominant influences leading to the increases in 'output'. Output was recorded automatically.

The method of choosing subjects was a little odd; two girls, who were reputed to be skilled at relay assembly, were asked to choose four others to work with them and the whole lot were segregated from the other 100 or so who were working on this particular job.

Full details of the different conditions in the Hawthorne

experiments have been written about ad nauseam (e.g. Viteles, 1954, Kelly, 1974) so they will not be repeated here; they are outlined below. Two of the periods are particularly relevant to the myths which have grown up around the Hawthorne experiments. These are period 7 and 12. In period 7 two of the subjects who were known as 1A and 1B had become rather obstreperous; their activities are described in great detail in Roethlisberger and Dixon (1939) and it seems their main offences were on the part of 1A to have got married and collectively to be very prone to talking!

Period	Condition	Duration weeks
1	Record of production of subjects without their knowledge in regular department	2
2	Introduction to test room	5
3	Change in method of payment	8
4	Two 5-min. rest periods, one a.m., one p.m.	5
5	Rest pauses increased to 10 min. each	4
6	Six 5-min. rest pauses	4
7	15-min. rest with lunch provided a.m.; 10-min. rest p.m.	11
8	Same as 7 but stopping at 16.30 hrs.	7
9	Same as 7 but stopping at 16.00 hrs	4
10	Back to condition 7	12
11	Same as 7 but with no Saturday work	9
12	Back to condition 3	12
13	Same as 7 but subjects provide own lunch	31
14	Same as 11	9
15–23	Same as 13	–

From quite an early stage in the experiment the amount of talking by the girls was worrying the investigators, because they felt that it meant that there was less attention being given to the work and that too much time was being spent in talking. So, twelve weeks after the girls had started in the test room, four out of the five of them were reprimanded by the foreman for talking too much. In the Hawthorne hierarchy a foreman was equivalent to a departmental supervisor and three ranks superior to the girls. Over the following twelve weeks the foreman made several further attempts to reduce what in his view was an excessive amount of talking. Periodically the amount of talking would increase with operators 1A and 2A being the ringleaders. An antagonism seems to have developed between these two girls and the test room authorities which went a good deal further than the 'talking problem'. According to the observers' records they were making a habit of coming back late from rest periods, complaining about the chairs, about the work which they were expected to do and even talking of going on strike. 'Any effort to reprimand them would bring the reply, "we thought you wanted us to work as we feel"'; after all, they had been told at the outset that they were to work at a natural pace and 'as they felt'. In period 7 operator 1A got married and there was a big increase in talking immediately before and after this event. Various attempts were made to curb the talking by getting the girls to call out every time they made an error. At the same time the operators in general and the two main miscreants in particular continued to be reproved and even to be threatened with the loss of their free lunches.

The experimenters had hoped that by putting a small group of girls into a special situation a 'spurt of cooperation' would develop which would ensure a normal and natural response to various experimental conditions. The experimenters did not make it very clear what they meant by this, but it seems probable that what they were looking for was an attitude on the part of the girls towards the experimenters and towards each other which could be treated as a constant factor in the experiment. This meant as Roethlisberger and Dixon (p. 54) put it 'the girls were to be "pure laboratory specimens", responding only to this and that arrangement of their working situation, uninfluenced by any factor which they could "willfully" control.'

It is hardly surprising that the experimenters came to view the behaviour of girls was approaching gross insubordination which was jeopardizing the success of their controlled experiment. At the end of period 7 the experimenters decided they had had enough, and the two girls were returned to the department from which they had come.

Since detailed output figures are not given anywhere in

Roethlisberger and Dixon one can only get a view by looking at their graphs, but it is fairly clear that the two girls were very much worse performers than the other three in the team, and it is claimed that there was considerable friction between these two and the other four girls, though this does not always come out clearly in the accounts which are given of the conversations in which the girls were involved. Be that as it may, the replacement of operators 1A and 2A by operators 1 and 2 made a radical change in the nature of the experiment.

The two new girls were selected by the foreman as being experienced and keen on taking part in the experiment. Immediately after their transfer into the test room they both produced an output, whether expressed as a total or as rate per hour, which was very much greater than anything that had been achieved by any of the original five girls when they first joined the test room and very much above the output achieved at any time by the two girls whom they replaced. Operator 2 was a twenty-one-year-old Italian whose mother died shortly after she had joined the test room and whose father became unemployed. She appeared to be a very strong character and rapidly assumed a leadership role in the group. Relationships with the experimenters which had become very poor during the incidents which led up to the sacking (Elton Mayo speaks of them as having 'dropped out' or that they 'retired'!) of the two operators gradually improved again, at any rate for a time. But as Carey (1967) says 'there would seem to be good grounds for supposing that supervision became more friendly and relaxed because output increased rather than vice versa'. Operator 2 wanted more money and she made quite sure that she got it and was supported by the other girls in her efforts.

In period 12, after a series of experiments on rest pauses and shortening the working week during which output and the rate of work steadily increased, the hours of work were returned to 48 which had been worked in periods 2 and 3; and surprise, surprise, *output went up again*; but the period of work had been increased by six hours, so it would have been very odd if it had not. What is more important is that the *rate* of work actually went down but was still higher than it had

61

been in periods 2 and 3. What actually did happen is open to some doubt. The results are given in two forms, average hourly output per week and total weekly output; then it is claimed that 'output' rose roughly 30 per cent, while on other occasions the term 'increase in output' is used. Although it is made clear elsewhere that what is meant is the rate of output per hour, it would seem that the claim of 30 per cent increase relates to total output, but even this is somewhat obscure.

It is clear from the account of the experiment that the girls heartily disliked the idea of going back to a 48-hour week with no rests, and their work deteriorated at once. They found various ways of wasting time, such as reading newspapers, eating candy and consequently getting thirsty and having to go repeatedly for drinks and, the old bugbear, talking and laughing. It is reported that the observer had discovered that the girls were deliberately trying to keep the output rate low (presumably this means rate per hour) so as to ensure that rest pauses would be reinstated. The friendly observer found himself dealing once again with excessive talking and with other deliberate time-wasting activities so that the experiment would be terminated; he used the technique of reprimand and threat, including the threat that the condition which the girls disliked so much would be continued for a much longer period. So the friendly supervision, on which Mayo and Roethlisberger placed such emphasis, appears to have ceased to be friendly as soon as the girls' output started to go down.

The discovery that a change to less favourable working conditions had nevertheless been accompanied by an increase of 'output' and that this 'output' was a great deal higher than it had been when the same conditions were tested in periods 2 and 3 was described by Chase (1941) in this rather extravagant description of what happened: 'The staff swooned at their desks. They thought they were returning the girls to the original conditions but found that those original conditions were gone for ever ... the experiment had changed under them, and the group they now had was not the group they had started with.' Although Chase did not mean it this way, what he said was strictly true, only three of the five girls who were there in the original conditions were remaining when period

12 commenced. This fact seems conveniently to have been forgotten by most of the commentators on the Hawthorne results which have given rise to the so-called 'Hawthorne effect'.

Under the influence of Elton Mayo the experimenters were very quick to claim that they were dealing with a social effect and they decided to check this finding by two further experiments. Stage II involved the setting up of a relay assembly test group in which five girls were simply shifted together in the main room and their method of incentive payment was changed so that they were paid a bonus on their own output instead of that of 100 girls. Production went up by 12 per cent on the base period but after protests from the remaining girls in the department they went back to the original method of payment and production fell like a soggy sponge to 95 per cent of base. Similar results were obtained in Stage III with another group, the mica-splitting test group in which the payment method remained unaltered, but the physical and organizational conditions of the relay assembly test room were replicated. Output went up 15·6 per cent in 14 months but there-thereafter declined. This was attributed to anxiety about the 'slump', which ultimately led to the end of the experiment and the sacking of the girls involved. The experimenters then made some extraordinary comparisons of non-comparable data and were reaffirmed in their belief that financial incentives played a very small part in this.

One possibility which has not been mentioned by any of the commentators is that the steady improvement in production may have been partly due to increasing skill on the part of the operatives. As Murrell (1971) has pointed out, learning can continue over a number of years and it is the establishment of a group norm which makes it appear that learning has reached an asymptote (or upper limit). In the relay assembly test room the restriction caused by the establishment of a norm did not seem to be present. It appears that over the time up to period 12 output in the main shop making relays had gone up 7 per cent and this could have been primarily due to improved skill; there is no reason to suppose that norms and output curtailment were not practised there as they were almost everywhere else, which could account for part of the differences between the improvement in the shop and in the test room. It seems highly probable that towards the end of the experiments, when the demand for the company's products started to fall off, at the beginning of the depression, the girls would slow down in order, as they hoped, to eke out the work as long as possible.

Experiments with wage incentives such as these would normally be taken as demonstrating efficacy of financial incentives, but Roethlisberger and Dixon seem to have been so sure that they were dealing with social factors that they would have none of this and came to the conclusion that 'none of the results gave the slightest substantiation to the theory that the worker is primarily motivated by economic interest. The evidence indicated that the efficacy of a wage incentive is so dependent on its relation to other factors that it is impossible to separate it out as a thing itself having an independent effect.'

Concurrently with Stages II and III, Stage IV of the Hawthorne investigation was the setting up of an extensive programme of interviewing using the 'unstructured' technique so much at the centre of the human relations movement at that time. All together some 20,000 employees were interviewed, and the most important thing they found was, to use Kelly's (1974) phrase, 'mafia-like' structures inside the primary working groups. 'These ... gangs (had) bosses and sidekicks who had built an elaborate social apparatus to ensure that just the right amount was produced.' In order to find out more about this informal organization and its workings a further experiment was set up which has become known as the Bank Wiring Observation Room. The task was the wiring of banks of terminals for use in telephone exchanges and nine wiremen, three soldermen and two inspectors were selected for the experiment and put in a separate room. It immediately became clear that, whatever the management did, the group had their own view of how much should be produced and the graph of output seemed to be a straight line. The mores of the group seemed to be that one must not turn out too much or too little work; one must not say anything to one's superiors that would harm an associate, and that one must conform to all the mandates of the informal group of which one is a part.

This was a remarkable discovery of something which had been known to management back in the mists of industrial history.

The experiment ran right on into the recession of the early thirties which caused its final abandonment, and it is noticeable that towards the end production began to decline. It may well be that towards the middle period trade was good (there is no record of this) and that there was pressure for higher production. Unfortunately, no production records for any of the individual operatives who were part of the experiment have been reported, so we do not know whether production also went up in the relay assembly department as a whole.

There is no doubt that this massive experiment triggered off a great deal of subsequent work and ideas, but at the same time it has been heavily criticized on a number of grounds.

Reports of the experiment appeared piecemeal, mainly in company reports, but in 1933 Mayo published a short but nevertheless reasonably comprehensive account. Commenting on the steady rise in production throughout the experiment and in particular performance in period 12, he says 'It had become clear that the ... changes experimentally imposed, although they could perhaps be used to account for minor differences between one period and another, yet could not be used to explain the major change – the continually increasing production. This steady increase ... seemed to ignore the experimental changes in its upward development.' It was this idea that the changes of production were due to something other than the changes in the experimental conditions, which was later developed more fully by Roethlisberger and Dixon when they published their detailed account of the experiments in 1939, which has come in for a good deal of scrutiny. One of the first in the field was Viteles (1932) who put forward the suggestion that there was slow adaptation to the experimental condition and that the experimental periods were not long enough for performance to have stablilized. He also pointed out that the output of two of the operators declined during the critical twelfth period. In a later book Viteles (1954) is a good deal more critical and much of what he said had been put forward by Argyle in 1953.

Other critics have included Landsberger (1958) who sets out to evaluate in almost a clinical atmosphere the various charges which have been made specifically against Roethlisberger and Dixon's presentation of the Hawthorne research, and against Elton Mayo and his school in their interpretation of the Hawthorne results. He makes the point that most of the criticism of the Mayo school is aimed not so much at what was done at Hawthorne, but at the expression of the school's ideology as set out in the writings of Mayo and others; and *Management and the Worker* has suffered by association. He then goes on to examine the Hawthorne studies under the title 'guilty as charged?' But he is less concerned with the actual experiments and the conclusions drawn from them than he is with other parts of the book dealing with the improvement of employee relations, the understanding of employee dissatisfaction and the social organization of employees. Two parts cannot however be separated since the latter sections have their foundations in the experimental programme. Landsberger's general conclusion seems to be that some charges are proven and some are not; that the actual book, *Management and the Worker,* has suffered by association with the other writings of the Mayo school. He also comes to the conclusion that the Hawthorne plant was a thoroughly unpleasant place to work in, and should not necessarily be considered as typical.

Carey (1967) in contrast deals more with the experiments and is far more devastating. He points out that the conclusions drawn are widely at variance with the evidence presented and that this evidence itself is unreliable. In the first place, it is not shown that the experimental periods were not responsible for all or part of the observed increase in output. Secondly, the disposal of two recalcitrant subjects and the introduction of two better workers made comparability between the periods before and after period 7 invalid. It is mentioned in several accounts that the new number 2 rapidly became the leader of of the group. Since she was the main financial support of her family she wanted high earnings: because of the method of payment she could only achieve these by pushing along the rest of the group at the same time. It is obviously impossible to quantify the extent of her influence. Thirdly, there was a reduction in the number of the types of relay which were being assembled and this was bound to have made the work easier. Thus the output per week showed a sustained increase only after the two recalcitrant operators had been got rid of, after the unpleasantness associated with their disciplining had had time to die down, and the influence of the two new operators, particularly number 2, had had time to establish itself. There was also a change in the method of payment in that the operators were now paid for time which was not worked, so that in effect piece-rate was increased. The general consensus of opinion seems to be that the so-called Hawthorne effect which seems to have almost universal acceptance stands on a very slender foundation indeed.

In his summary of his paper Carey, after pointing out that the conclusions drawn from Hawthorne are almost entirely unsupported by the evidence, asks how it was 'possible for studies so nearly devoid of scientific merit, and conclusions so little supported by evidence to gain so influential and respected a place within the scientific disciplines and to hold this place for so long.'

Kelly (1974) expressed much the same view when he said 'the most perplexing and worrying aspect ... is why studies which exercise so much influence on the thinking of social scientists, executives and social reformers were not subjected to the most searching and sceptical scrutiny. Why did most authors of text books and most teachers of courses on organization theory fail to recognize the discrepancy between Hawthorne evidence and Hawthorne conclusions? ... For their conclusions set the tone of the social science organizations for a generation.'

This then is in outline what happened at Hawthorne and some of the curious conclusions which were drawn from the experiments; both the validity of the experiments themselves and of the conclusions drawn from them have been severely challenged. It is quite clear that although the experiments were launched with quite an open mind the experimenters' ideas became so completely fossilized that everything else they did seems to have been done with the object of proving that they were right rather than conducting an enquiry with an open mind. The consequence was that even when they were staring them in the face, results which contradicted their preconceived ideas were ignored. Any reader who wishes to go into the matter further either for interest or amusement should study the references given in the text.

We have now looked at two experiments, one British and one American, which were carried out with much the same objectives. Of the two, the British work appeared to be much more rigorous and has not been subject to the same level of criticism. On the other hand, the results have not been widely publicized. In contrast, the American experiments which were very sloppy were given enormous and largely undeserved publicity. The British experiment was one of an ongoing series and was published as an official government report. The American work was written up in a series of books and was used as propaganda for a preconceived school of thought and is still even now the subject of controversy. Perhaps it doesn't pay to be too rigorously scientific!

4
Research associated activities – post-1939

Before 1939, as we have seen, the main development of motivation and incentives emanated from industry itself with the social sciences rather tagging along behind. The main characteristic of the post-1939 period is the emergence of the social scientists in general and psychologists in particular as an influence in the industrial scene. Because of the impact of some of the ideas put forward by various psychologists on management thinking, the order of presentation will be the reverse of that used to cover the pre-1939 period. This is not meant to imply that everything that management did in the post-1939 period was the result of psychologists entering into the industrial field; in fact it was not until about the middle 1960s when industry in general, with its economists and accountants, had become barren of ideas that the social scientists began to make any very real impact. But to understand their application it is necessary to look at the theories first.

Theories of needs

'Classical' psychological views of motivation were expressed in terms of a collection of separate and distinct drives (see D2). An alternative view was put forward by Maslow, first in 1943 and then further developed in 1954, who postulated a hier-

69

archy of needs which means that for most people there is an order of priority, which may differ from individual to individual, of those matters which each considers to be important. This priority will vary at different stages of an individual's life.

The use of the term 'need' has been criticized by Blackler and Williams (1971) who point out that it has two meanings. First it is used as a technical term by people like Hull to refer to a state which can be measured independently from the behaviour which is initiated to change it. But in every day language it is used to emphasize things which are important to people without saying why this should be so. 'One may say "he needed the money", and "need" here is used to point out that money was a powerful motive for the individual concerned; it does *not* refer to any state that is identified individually from behaviour.' The predisposition of psychologists to use ordinary words to mean different things, a point which was commented on in the introduction, is indeed unfortunate. In this area also it has led to a good deal of confusion, with Hull meaning one thing, Maslow something different, Herzberg something else and the man in the street something different yet again. Kelly (1974) has suggested that 'needs' are the first step in a chain; they cause 'drives' which determine behaviour aimed at reaching a 'goal' which leads to reduction or release of 'tension' (whatever this may be). The modern systems approach would define a need as a system requirement which must be met if the system is to function satisfactorily.

The history of research by early psychologists for a theory of motivation has been clearly summarized by Viteles (1954). After a period when theories concentrated on 'instinct' as a basis for motivation, motives themselves were described and classified as 'primary' or 'secondary' (see D2); the primary motives are those which serve some biological function, while the secondary motives were largely social. The next step was to identify motives with 'needs' and to substitute these in the dichotomy which was called by a variety of names such as 'biogenic' and 'psychogenic'; 'super-ordinate' and 'sub-ordinate'; 'pheno-motives' and 'geno-motives'. Murry (1938) suggested that within these two groups there were differences in the order of strength or 'prepotency' of the motives. Maslow's contribution was to disregard the dichotomy and to rank needs in a hierarchy of prepotency in which he put the biological needs as those which had to be satisfied first before other, higher needs could receive attention. Underlying all this early theory of motivation is the idea of the existence of 'tension' or disequilibrium which an individual seeks to restore to a state of rest or balance (Kornhausser, 1939). In some theories the term 'tension-system' is used as a synonym for 'need'.

Maslow divided his hierarchy of needs into five categories:

1. Physiological needs, such as hunger, thirst and sex which are basic requirements for survival.
2. Safety needs, such as security and freedom from threat.
3. The need to belong, such as love and affection, acceptance by others.
4. Esteem needs, such as self respect, success.
5. The need for 'self-actualization', such as self-fulfilment, identity or achievement of one's full potential.

By placing these needs in a hierarchy Maslow suggested that a lower need must be filled before the next higher need can emerge and so on down the list. The stark simplicity of this proposition sometimes led to a rigidity of view which was no part of Maslow's hypothesis, since Maslow believed that an individual's hierarchy of needs must be viewed as a whole in order to understand his behaviour. The hierarchy will not necessarily be the same for all individuals or for people of different ages, but underlying all possible variation is the fundamental view that a lower need must be satisfied before the next higher need can emerge.

Maslow's theory has been received with approval by a number of psychologists, and it forms the basis of theories of motivation taught in business schools, particularly in North America, and for much organization theory. Acceptance of the theory in this way is largely an act of faith since very little research has been done to verify it. There have been a number of findings which can be interpreted in terms of Maslow's model (and probably other models as well) but as Blackler and Williams (1971) point out 'interpretation is quite different from testing. And this is the crunch as far as Maslow is concerned; it has proved easy to interpret situations by his model, rather more elusive to actually test it out'.

There are features in applying Maslow's theory which make application in the industrial situation somewhat difficult. Lower needs are not constant and, since they must be satisfied before higher needs are dealt with, motivation to achieve at higher levels must fluctuate in a complex sort of way. And if the lower needs are not satisfied when do they become deprivations and in turn real threats? Maslow gives no real guidance on this point, which means that his theory is not much help in the formulation of practical predictions. Maslow is also criticized by Blacker and Williams (1971) on the grounds that his findings may apply to a particular sector of American society with which he was in contact, but no evidence has been produced to show that it relates to anybody else. To use Maslow's jargon, 'perhaps some people "self-actualize" through their social relations ... perhaps some people find that satisfactory social relations ... are worthy goals to be aimed at in their own right.' They come to the conclusion that Maslow's model is misleading.

Another difficulty is in relation to job satisfaction, since in theory a satisfied employee should be better motivated to produce. But it can be argued that if job satisfaction is high, then all Maslow's hierarchy of needs has been satisfied, and the individual will be no longer motivated. On the other hand members of the 'needs school' seem to believe that the development of motivation is a prerequisite of job satisfaction, which makes one wonder whether once again the psychological theorists are using words to mean something different to the understanding of the common man. And in any event, it must be recognized that we have a concept which, even in its normal use by industrialists, is woolly in the extreme. When an industrialist talks about job satisfaction he has some overt behaviour in mind which he can confirm or refute after his fashion; it is almost certainly not true of the theoretical psychologist.

A second theory based on human needs has been put forward by Herzberg *et al* (1959) and developed in Herzberg (1968). Herzberg's original investigation was carried out by a survey of a comparatively small number of engineers and accountants in Pittsburgh using the *critical incident* technique administered through semi-structured interviews. As a result he discovered that when asked to describe times when they were satisfied at work, people seemed to be describing factors such as achievement, advancement, recognition, responsibility and the nature of the work itself; when asked to describe the more dissatisfying situations, they spoke of factors such as company policy, supervision, relations with superiors, working conditions and pay. Herzberg concluded that the first group were motivators whereas the second group were not; if any of the conditions were adverse they would cause a climate of dissatisfaction, but they did not act as motivators when conditions were good. This is a very puzzling idea since the ordinary man would assume that the *presence or absence* of a certain factor (say good pay) would give rise to *satisfaction or dissatisfaction*, whereas Herzberg, in effect, is saying that a high level of pay is not a motivator. Herzberg called this second group of factors 'hygiene factors'. Once again we have an example of psychologists using a common word in an unusual way which can cause amongst the uninitiated some ribaldry such as 'wash your hands after going to the lavatory'. Thus, in effect, he reduced Maslow's hierarchy of needs to two factors, the hygiene factors relating to the first two needs and the motivators relating to the last three; the theory has therefore become known as the 'two-factor theory' or the 'M-H theory'.

The two sets of factors are not opposites; it does not matter how interesting or challenging a job may be, poor pay or working conditions will still cause dissatisfaction. The opposite is also true; it does not matter how good are the working conditions; they will not produce motivation or satisfaction, which can only come from a rewarding job. The value of the two-factor theory lies in its concentration on the motivational importance of the task vis-a-vis the environment, a view which is almost directly contrary to most current thinking in industry, which is to reduce most tasks to their component parts and to concentrate attempts at motivation on pay and similar benefits. It is not surprising therefore that two-factor theory caused a good deal of interest and excitement both among occupational psychologists and the managements of, usually, the larger companies. There are those who obviously feel that Herzberg's ideas are unquestionably right and who seek to promote his theories, but there are others who are nothing like so convinced. Its main practical outcome is 'job enrichment', but, as we have pointed out (see p. 30) practical men acting empirically had already successfully 'enriched' jobs more than seventy years earlier. Even Herzberg's strongest critics would have to admit that, whether his theory holds water or not, his convincingly presented material in *Work and the Nature of Man* has reawakened attention in, and created some enthusiasm for, job enrichment. As Paul and Robertson (1970) put it 'the message of the theory is clear: no amount of environmental improvement can compensate for task impoverishment. If we are concerned to motivate people, we must look again at the tasks we ask them to do.' Now anyone who has actually worked in industry for real, particularly if they were on the shop floor, will know that this statement is only partially true and, this being so, Herzberg's two-factor theory loses a good deal of its utility. Both Herzberg himself and others have carried out a number of studies to test the validity of his theory, and all those who have used his basic technique have produced similar results; but those who have used other methods have failed to confirm Herzberg's findings. Kelly (1974) says that one thing which is certain from results of research using Herzberg's techniques is that his motivators apply far more to management than they do to supervisors, and that they apply even less to the shop floor. Since it is on the shop floor that most of the action is, the idea that you can ignore the so-called 'hygiene' factors could be quite dangerous.

House and Wigdor (1968) reviewed approximately forty studies which were critical of the two-factor theory on four main grounds. First, the theory is methodologically 'egg bound'; Vroom (1964) has suggested that when things are going well, people will tend to put themselves in the best light, but when they are describing a situation when things are going badly, they will protect their self-images by blaming failure on to the environment or on to others. So as long as the critical incident technique is used the results will always be biased data. Secondly, the responses are evaluated by a rater, and this could lead to rater bias (we have already seen what could happen with people with preconceived ideas in our discussion of the Hawthorne experiments). Thirdly, no overall measure of satisfaction was used. Most people may well dislike some features in their job but may still find the job highly acceptable. Finally, the theory is at variance with other research which does not suggest that the environmental variables play an important role in any relationship between motivation and productivity. House and Wigdor come to the conclusion that the two-factor theory is an oversimplification of a very complex relationship between motivation, satisfaction and job performance. As a postscript: in his monumental and authoritative book *Management* Peter Drucker, the international authority on management practice (1974), accords Herzberg a couple of lines in two places and a footnote!

Management styles

Workers, whether they are motivated or otherwise, are inevitably functioning within a management organization. The means by which needs are met do not just materialize, they are provided by an organization (see B4). The proposal which links Maslow's needs to reality came from McGregor (1960) in Theory X and Theory Y. In his purely theoretical exposition, McGregor equates Theory X with a 'carrot-and-stick' style of management which assumes that people are lazy, that they dislike and shun work and have to be driven to be productive. In contrast Theory Y, which owes a good deal to Drucker (1950), assumes a psychological need to work, to want to achieve and to accept responsibility. Theory X can be equated (as were Herzberg's hygiene factors) with the first two of Maslow's hierarchy of needs, while Theory Y can be equated with the other three. McGregor's theory is often regarded as a practical extention of Maslow's theories, and Maslow himself became an ardent enthusiast for Theory Y, as also clearly was McGregor, although he went through the motions of being impartial.

Theory X sums up the traditional style of management, which seems to have worked on the assumption that the average individual prizes security above everything; prefers to be told what to do; does not like taking responsibility; has relatively little ambition. The popular philosophy of management by direction and control will not motivate work-people because of the low level of the needs on which they depend. The difference between Theory X and Theory Y is not the difference between 'hard' and 'soft' management; in other words a change of management style simply by removing control will not be successful; abdication is not a workable alternative to authoritarianism and Theory Y does not imply that management has become permissive. On the contrary, Theory Y management is quite tough, and can make very high demands on both the manager and the managed. Maslow (1965), after a year spent working with a company which was trying to practice Theory Y, pointed out that demands made by the theory are such that only the tough and strong can take them. Theory Y assumes an enterprise peopled by adults, but Maslow points out that it will also have its share of the permanently immature, and he accuses McGregor of inhumanity to those who are not sufficiently strong to take on the responsibility and the self-discipline which Theory Y demands.

Whether or not there is scientific validity in Theory X or Theory Y, it is an inescapable fact that the carrot-and-stick type of management no longer works and that an alternative, whether you call it Theory Y or anything else, has got to be found. Many enterprises are groping towards alternatives and may use the ideas of Theory Y as a guide.

A classification similar in concept but very different in approach was being developed concurrently by Likert (1961, 1967) who postulated *four styles of management* ranging from System 1, exploitive-authoritative, through System 2, benevolent-authoritative, System 3, consultative, to System 4, participative. System 1 can be equated with Theory X while System 4 can be equated with Theory Y. The main difference between the two is that McGregor produced theories without making any attempt at their validation whereas, covering a similar area, Likert has produced postulates which can be validated. With the aid of an extensive inventory which is completed by individuals in a company, profiles for that company in relation to the four systems can be prepared. This can be either of the management systems as it actually is or, as the participants desire that it should be. In companies which come under the influence of Likert's ideas the object is for the reality to become closer to the ideal. One company which is discussed in great detail is the Harwood Manufacturing Company which is described in the next chapter, and in particular the changes which took place when Harwood's management system was gradually introduced into its former competitor, the Weldon Company, which it had just taken over. Over a period of two years there had been a very marked shift from a profile somewhere between System 1 and System 2 to a profile which was clearly System 3. The old management at Weldon had obviously learned their lessons because the system which they desired after two years was very clearly System 4. Over the same period there was an increase in productivity of 26 per cent, most of which is attributed to the change in management style.

In the last two sections we have looked at four approaches to motivation, three mainly theoretical and one more practical. All have in common the idea of participation, relying on everyone in an organization to take responsibility which is appropriate to the job which he is doing. But most of these theoreticians are looking in from the top down. There is no doubt that most top managers are well motivated if they are professional rather than hereditary, but what of those lower down? The top echelons of middle management may also be well motivated, but for those on the lower rungs of the management ladder, the superintendents, the foremen, the charge hands, these new styles of management may cause many problems. This is discussed more fully in the next chapter. It is in relation to the shop floor that the theorists are at their weakest. System 4 or Theory Y may work to some extent in jobs which are basically machine minding, as they seem to have done with nylon spinning which is described in the next chapter, but not always in accordance with theory. When work is more repetitive there seems to be much greater resistance in many

77

trades, partly for historic reasons, partly from sheer bloody-minded inertia and partly because, as Maslow says, a proportion of every community is permanently adolescent and just does not want to take any responsibility. It is quite clear that we are still a very long way from understanding how motivation at work works.

Rest pauses and social interaction

The idea that rest is an integral part of work and should be taken at predetermined intervals goes right back to Taylor, but Bedaux changed the concept by giving a rest allowance as a percentage of the rate for the job. From the writings of the times, it is clear that in the 1920s operatives were expected to work for long periods, up to four and a half to five hours, without any rest at all. In 1925 Hersey says that in the coil-winding department of a textile mill, where 50 girls (aged 13 to 22) worked a nine and three-quarter hour day, the foreman complained that the 'sneak to the toilet' was the bane of his existence. 'So prevalent was the trouble that he could pick out no one person not guilty. Recognizing that the length of the working period justified some trips to the dressing room, he could devise no standard rule to apply without incurring the risk of encroaching too heavily upon his workers' actual rights.' He gives another example of five girls in a plant where no authorized rests were allowed, who admitted that when the forewoman would not 'let them sneak off', they found ways of putting their machines temporarily out of order. Any rests they were able to take were spent in the only place that was, and often still is, available, the lavatory. These were the kinds of conditions extant when the investigators of the Industrial Fatigue Research Board started looking at the incidence of rest pauses, and Wyatt was able to summarize a quite extensive programme by 1927.

The IFRB investigators used the beginning of a decrement of performance as an indicator that the time was ripe for a rest. When Murrell in 1962 started an extensive study into fatigue in light repetitive work he used a different criterion.

Barlett (1953) had suggested, without experimental foundation, that the first indication of psychological fatigue would be the appearance of irregularity in the sequence of repetitive motions. Murrell, using a technique borrowed from quality control, demonstrated that this indeed did happen (Murrell and Forsaith, 1963). The appearance of irregularity was preceded by a period of regular performance which Murrell (1962) has called the actile period; a break given at the end of an actile period was found to be more beneficial than a break taken when output had begun to fall. Breaks taken voluntarily were usually taken well after the end of the actile period and were found to be less beneficial (Murrell, 1965).

An implication of these findings is that in repetitive or non-repetitive monotonous work it is best for management to arrange a work–rest schedule which is suitable for the type of work being done – best both for the firm and for the operatives. An extensive experiment was carried out in a small section, welding account book covers for Kalamazoo Ltd (Bhatia and Murrell, 1969). Two schedules of work and rest were used; in the first there were three ten-minute breaks in the morning and in the afternoon, for the second there were two fifteen minute breaks in each period. The total rest was therefore one hour out of eight, equivalent to a rest allowance of $12\frac{1}{2}$ per cent. The women involved were interviewed before the beginning of the experiment, at the end of schedule 1, and at the end of schedule 2. Schedule 1 lasted for eighteen weeks and schedule 2 for seven weeks. The operatives disliked schedule 2 and asked to go back on to schedule 1, which lasted for a further five weeks. On schedule 1 the mean efficiency index, allowed time divided by time actually taken, went up approximately 4 per cent (this depended on the accuracy of the setting of time values). Average earnings went up 7 per cent. On schedule 2 the efficiency index was $2\frac{1}{2}$ per cent up, but earnings were very slightly down.

Kalamazoo was an interesting firm in that the majority of the shares were owned by a workers' trust. But this did not mean that the operatives who took part in the experiment had any real feeling of 'owning' the firm. It was clear that there was virtually no restriction of output and there was no belief that if output went up rates would be cut. Quite apart from the increase in production and earnings it became abundantly clear that one of the things which the operatives really liked was the opportunity for social interaction every fifty minutes. An important feature of the experiment was that the firm had provided, within twenty seconds walk of the work place, a rest room where the operatives could spend their ten-minute breaks and where refreshment was available from a vending machine. From conversation with the girls it was clear that one of the things they liked about the new system was the fact that they knew they could spend fifty minutes of uninterrupted work and then have their ten minutes of social contact. With the old system, which applies almost everywhere, where operatives were allowed to take a rest whenever they wished, the girls never seemed to go to the lavatory singly; they always seemed to go in pairs, or, in some factories even in triplets. This means that if one girl decides that she wishes to pay a visit, she will go and collect her friend and will often stop and speak to any other girl who happens to be in the line of flight. This can cause irritation to the people interrupted and, where the job is complex, can cause faulty products. Since these breaks are officially for personal reasons, the girls are usually not permitted to go to the canteen, so that all their socializing takes place in the lavatory which is hardly one of the most salubrious of places! It is this provision of somewhere close to the place of work to which operatives can go during their rest period, coupled with an organization which allows a period of uninterrupted work as well as periods of rest, which makes the kind of organization which was tested at Kalamazoo highly acceptable.

There is no doubt that if management does not make provision for socializing during the working period the operatives will make opportunities themselves, usually in a disruptive sort of way. If management makes proper provision and openly recognizes that official contact is an important part of the working environment, the effect on the work-force cannot be anything but good. This was demonstrated recently during a consultancy, where machines were moved together so that the girls could talk and the girls were told why it was done. As the girls had no longer to stop work and get up to go and talk to another girl, there was an increase in production of about 7 per cent without any adverse effect on quality. No formal measurement of opinion was taken, but a number of the girls involved went out of the way to say how much they preferred the new arrangement. Naturally, care was taken to make sure that the girls who were close together were friends and not enemies.

Flexible working hours

Flexible working hours is a scheme which lies part way between the tight system imposed by the time clock and its complete abandonment. It originated in Germany at the end of the 1960s, and has been marketed with a special form of time clock under the name of 'Flexitime'. The basic idea is that there is a core of hours which must be worked by everybody, but on either side of this core individuals are free to come and go when they wish within certain limits. Over a specified period the correct total of hours must be worked; in some systems a carry-over is permitted whereas in others it is not. A minimum compulsory lunch break is enforced.

The effect of introducing flexible working hours into two offices has been described. In one office the core time was from 1000 to 1600, with flexible bands two hours on either side. The original starting hour had been 08.30. When the new system was in operation more than half the staff were in by 08.15 and 86 per cent by 08.30. The lunch break had previously been one hour and the compulsory minimum had come down to half an hour; it was clear that most staff were taking advantage of this reduction because a noticeable difference was seen at the end of the day when, by 16.15, 20 per cent had left already and, by 17.30 which was the original ending time, only one-third of the staff was still there.

The attitude to flexible working hours was assessed on a 7 point scale. On one dimension, running from strongly in favour to strongly against, 67 per cent were strongly in favour with 90 per cent responding on the positive side of the mid-point.

There was none strongly against. On the dimension of convenience, 63 per cent found it much more convenient and again 90 per cent were on the positive side of the mid-point, with none finding the scheme much less convenient. In a further study to determine the importance of other features in the job relative to flexible working hours, it was found that there were twelve features which were considered to be more important such as pay (at the top), security of employment, the amount of responsibility, the variety of work, promotion prospects, and so on. Features which were considered less important were such things as the quality of the office accommodation, the welfare arrangements, and the canteen facilities. It seems very clear that although flexible working hours were liked by a large majority of people involved, it was not highly regarded as a feature of the job; once again pay has come out at the top as being much more important. An extensive review of flexible working hours has been carried out by Wade (1973).

5
Motivation by management - post-1939

For most people in most countries World War Two produced the greatest upheaval that mankind had ever known. Anyone who said 'things will never quite be the same again' was making the understatement of the century; things would never begin to be even approximately the same again. A high proportion of men who had been normally engaged in industry and commerce had found a new type of life in the armed forces, sometimes a very exciting if somewhat brutalized new life, while women were doing almost all the jobs which hitherto had been considered to be a male prerogative. Moreover, unlike World War One, a majority of those who had experienced an escape from the tyranny of the production line would return to their old jobs with a very different point of view and attitude. They came back with a newfound independence and a disinclination to be pushed around. Quite soon industry was building up its productive effort to replace the losses of five years of war; everyone had a job, and the myth of full employment was born. The workers were beginning to feel that they now had a stake in the means of production and should have a say in the way things were run.

The state was not the only body to become a large employer. Firms started to amalgamate or were taken over, and the pace at which this happened has been steadily increasing ever since, with the result that the top management is becoming increasingly remote from those engaged in production. When enterprise was becoming more monolithic, it is not surprising that the unions followed much the same course. Not only have they stepped up recruitment of members, enforced wherever possible by the closed shop, but they have themselves amalgamated into larger and larger groups. As a consequence, with the centres of power and decision moving further and further away from each other, it became increasingly difficult for either side of industry to talk to the other as individuals.

A consequence of all these changes has been that management no longer had the sanctions which it was able to exercise before the war; it was progressively losing authority and power, and it was less and less able to deal with its work-force as individuals. In negotiation they were having to deal with increasingly larger groups, and their attempts to achieve high production by peaceable means were frustrated by the unions who have a vested interest in conflict – not that conflict is always a bad thing.

The changes that have been described have been taking place progressively over the thirty years since the war ended. They were not something which suddenly happened at a single stroke in 1945, but as industry started getting into its stride again management found that the techniques of motivation which it practised before the war would no longer work. So the last thirty years have seen a succession of different management techniques which have become fashionable for a short time, and then when something which appeared to be better came along were dropped in its favour, and so on; the whole sorry sequence has been set out in the introduction. Setting out the sequence in this way is not meant to imply that each panacea fits into a neat compartment with one terminating as another starts. The boundaries are quite blurred with some techniques continuing, to a greater or lesser extent, throughout the postwar period. But what the sequence does imply is that there was a sudden upsurge or interest in one technique after another.

The first management fashion was *joint consultation* which had its roots pre-war but which burgeoned in the early forties with governmental encouragement. It was still believed that it was possible to treat the work-force as individuals and to consult with them; the blanketing effect of organized labour had not yet sunk in. There was a very compelling need to tap the 'will to work' in order to raise production to something like that of which the work-force was capable. As far back as 1934 Strong had stated that 'a few, if any, employees were working up to their capacity', much the same conclusion has been reached by Murrell in 1971. While this attitude might be understandable during the slump it seems scarcely credible in an era of relatively full employment and prosperity. An American enquiry found that approximately 55 per cent of managements of all types and sizes of companies stated that they had experienced a decrease in productivity in their factories after World War Two. This was reinforced by Henry Ford II who has said that the Ford Motor Company in America was getting about one-third less output in the immediate post-war years than it did in 1941 per man hour on comparable products. The General Motors Corporation reported a slightly larger drop in productivity. So management was faced with a disturbing situation and the first panacea to which some of them turned was joint consultation.

It is impossible to say exactly how extensive joint consultation was. The NIIP (1952) carried out a wide-ranging enquiry in 1948–9 into the extent of joint consultation in British industry. They sent out questionnaires to 4,719 manufacturing establishments each employing more than 250 people; 751 replied, of which 545 had joint consultation. In their report they give a detailed account of the practices which they found in a sample of 157 factories, but they do not give detailed case studies of what happened in particular firms. There are, however, two outstanding examples which are widely reported, one from America and the other from Britain. In one the consultation is flexible and informal and in the other it is more proscribed. The organizations are the Harwood Manufacturing Company and Glacier Metals.

The Harwood Manufacturing Company

Harwood must have been almost unique in having a president who was the holder of a Ph.D. in psychology. Alfred J. Marrow took up his appointment in a family firm which manufactured clothing in 1937 very shortly after obtaining his doctorate. Just prior to Marrow taking over, the firm moved into a country district in Virginia; productivity was so low in the new location and labour turnover so high that the very existence of the company was threatened. After conventional ways of discovering what was wrong had been tried, Marrow asked the German psychologist, Kurt Lewin, to come to the factory to see what he could find out. It soon became clear that the greatest losses were in the trainees who were attempting to reach the production norm, the highest loss being amongst those who had nearly got there but could not quite make it. The problem was solved by establishing a series of intermediate targets with adequate recognition and reward. All this has nothing to do with joint consultation, but it was the means of introducing psychologists into the plant to carry out investigations of one sort or another which continued for more than thirty years.

Much of this work has been described by Marrow *et al* 1967. The method of employee participation adopted at Harwood was basically informal and was called 'participative management' which, Marrow explains, is not a set of rules but an attitude which encourages a sharing between management and employees in establishing objectives, in making decisions and in problem solving. The technique is based on the well-established psychological principle that a person will be more strongly motivated to achieve a goal which he has helped to establish himself than when it has been established by a superior. The objectives were not by any manner of means philanthropic. The firm has its eye firmly set on profitability as well as on making the company satisfying to work for.

As we have said the participation was informal and groups were set up as required to deal with particular problems. The powers of these groups varied considerably. Sometimes they could make firm decisions, on other occasions consent to a decision had to be obtained, while on yet other occasions advice only was asked for and this might not necessarily be followed.

As far as possible the whole exercise proceeded experimentally. For example, being in the fashion business, styles would change and so would production methods, new piece-work rates would have to be established. The problem was tackled with the classical device of an experimental group and a control group. The experimental group held meetings at which the requirements for the changes were explained and suggestions for cost reduction or method improvement were asked for from the workers. After a training period the experimental group reached its level of production within two days and after three weeks exceeded it by 14 per cent. But the control group which had simply had a change imposed upon it showed a fall of 35 per cent in production and nearly one fifth of the operatives left within forty days.

As so often happens with shop-floor experiments, holes can be picked, and this experiment has not escaped criticism. Be that as it may, the experiment was considered to be a success. Marrow's philosophy was that when an idea had been proved to work, it should be used as a management technique. This enabled the firm to achieve major and fundamental changes in the piece-work system by giving the operatives a full under-standing of why the changes were being made and full partici-pation in planning and carrying them out. It also enabled them to carry out major changes in management and shop-floor practices when Harwood took over its major competitor.

The Glacier Metal Company

By contrast, joint consultation in the Glacier Metal Company was formal. The main driving force behind the establishment of joint consultation was Wilfred Brown, a Scot with experi-ence in accountancy who joined the company in 1931 and was its managing director and chairman from 1939 to 1965. Glacier was the largest manufacturer of plain bearings in Europe. In 1948 Brown was approached by Elliot Jaques, a

Canadian psychiatrist, on the staff at the Tavistock Institute for Human Relations. Thus began a curious relationship between Tavistock in general and Jaques in particular and Glacier which lasted for many years.

The initial impetus for the collaboration between Brown and Jaques was primarily to investigate how the worker committees might be made more effective. From this developed the system of management by consultation for which Glacier has become famous (Brown, 1960). Brown believed that in addition to a man's right to abundant employment and to equitable payment he should also have the right to participate fully in policy making and in defining the areas of managerial authority. He should also have the right of appeal against a management decision. The management system at Glacier as it evolved secured these last two rights. Brown (1972) writing later confirms his belief that what he calls the 'employment hierarchy' is the most effective way of getting things done in an enterprise. On this score 'democratic' systems such as are implied by 'workers' control' and arrangements by which no-one has authority over anyone else are likely to be hopelessly inefficient and would only lead to an unacceptable reduction in 'living standards'.

So the Glacier system still maintained a hierarchy of authority (subject to appeal) with participation by the workforce in policy making. Thus the government of Glacier was based on three systems: an executive system, a representative system and a legislative system. In addition there was the right of appeal. At the top of the executive system was the general manager and below him three staff grades represented by unit managers, section managers, supervisors. Below this in the hierarchy were the workers on the shop floor. The representatives system consisted of three committees, one for each grade, which appointed representatives of the Works Council, the legislative body. Each production unit within the organization had its own unit committee which sent representatives to the Works Committee which in turn was represented on the Works Council by the shop stewards. Each of these committees deliberated and made decisions on matters which were relevant to their own group but passed on to the

Works Council those matters which would affect others than themselves. Since 1949 the Works Council has been the policy making body for the whole company, representatives from all parts of the organization joining together in the making of all major policy decisions. A unique feature of the operation of the Works Council was that all decisions had to be unanimous, and so the representatives of each group had in effect a veto on policy decisions which it would not lightly use. This demanded a sense of responsibility which would rarely be found in situations where a representative could vote against a motion knowing perfectly well that it would be carried and put into effect. This is very close to the quaker philosophy of making all decisions by consensus and without voting. In this manner policy making and executive action were separated. Management's job was to run the concern in accordance with the laid down policy, and in this respect the Glacier technique differed from the more common approach to joint consultation where both the policy and the executive action remained the prerogative of management and consultation largely consisted of discussing with representatives of the shop floor how the proposed policies would be carried out. Joint consultation in the normally accepted sense is very rarely a policy making function. The final feature of the system was the right of appeal against managerial decisions. This meant that some-body on the shop floor who felt aggrieved by a decision of his supervisor could appeal to his section manager and so on up the hierarchy.

In the process of transforming Glacier into a participative organization a number of other important changes were made. Foremen were re-named section managers and given rather wider duties as well as enhanced status, but for them as for their immediate superiors there were a number of problems which were stubborn to resolve. These are discussed more fully below. Employees were no longer required to clock in, and the use of financial incentives in the form of piece-work was ended (Brown, 1960).

Glacier, intensively studied and widely reported, has a standing in industrial folklore equal to if not greater than Hawthorne. Hawthorne achieved relatively little for itself but provided the spark which set off Elton Mayo's contentious human relations school. Glacier achieved a lot for itself but, in spite of Wilfred Brown's efforts, it has not inspired a flowering of participation. Brown firmly believes that the findings of Glacier can be applied nationally and he set out his ideas in 1972 in *The Earnings Conflict*.

Harwood and Glacier have in common that both developed the idea of participation and both were highly successful without sacrificing conventional authority or standards of earnings productivity and profits. But here similarities end. At Harwood the participation was informal, as and when required, with groups being formed from the shop floor, the supervisors and executives. There was no formal policy making, although consultation undoubtedly did lead to the formulation of policy. In contrast Glacier had a formal structure with the Works Council as its focus. This can cause us to wonder just what joint consultation or participation really are. The answer probably is that it is not so much what is done but who does it. In both firms there was a quite unusual chief executive, each of whom teamed up with an equally unusual psychologist. It was this rather rare symbiotic combination which seems to have been the key to the success in these two firms. The fact that such a combination is very rare probably accounts for the comparatively short-lived interest in participation as a motivator by industry as a whole.

The golden age of incentives

Towards the end of the 1940s three circumstances combined to give a tremendous fillip to financial incentives. The first of these was great pressure exerted by the government on firms to increase productivity. They tried to do this in the only way they knew, by offering greater financial rewards. The second was the growth of the consultant firms. Some of these had existed during the war when their activities had been mainly concerned with problems of training, such as for instance the training of women to take over men's jobs in engineering; when the war ended most of this work suddenly dried up, so they had to find something else to do and they turned to the installation of bonus schemes which in the deplorable state of post-war management and industrial organization were sure-fire winners. At the same time there was strong commercial development of synthetics under such titles as Methods Time Measurement or Work Factor. These originated in America and very rapidly found a strong foothold in Britain. The third factor was the consolidaion of a method of operation based on Bedaux concepts (see p. 35) and given the name of Work Study by Imperial Chemical Industries. In due time the practice of work study emerged as a recognized profession internationally with a consequent standardization of techniques.

With such a wide use of financial incentives it was natural that their efficiency should be investigated if not questioned. On the one hand were people, exemplified by P. S. Florence of Birmingham University, who gave unqualified support, and on the other hand psychologists like Viteles who are much more cautious and questioning. Florence in his writings has given many examples of substantial increases in productivity resulting, so he claimed, from the introduction of financial incentives. But in practically every instance the introduction of incentives was accompanied by changes in method so that it is impossible to say how much improvement was due to the incentives and how much to the change – so long as production went up perhaps it did not matter very much.

It will be remembered that after the war the IHRB was continued in part as the Industrial Psychology Research Group, some members of which became involved in an assessment of the motivating effect of financial incentives. In his introduction, Marriott (1968) said that the government had suggested that in order to double the standard of living within twenty-five years, productivity should increase by about 3 per cent per annum compound. To achieve this everyone in industry 'would have to be highly motivated to contribute as fully as necessary to achieve such an objective'. Motivation in industry thus began to receive particular attention as an issue of great importance. ... One of the major forms of motivation traditional in industrial operations' is the use of financial incentives. The actual investigations were initiated by the Joint Committee on Human Relations in Industry of the MRC and the Department of Scientific Industrial Research. A summary of the available information with a critical appraisal was published by Marriott (1968), with a notable contribution also coming from Shimmin who carried out investigations of her own (Shimmin, 1955, 1959). The general conclusion from their work seems to be that although the methods used are easily faulted, in practice they do work after their fashion.

The basic assumption underlying all the incentive payment schemes is that it is possible to measure work accurately enough to ensure that a worker is paid strictly according to the results of his efforts. Thus time study is supposed to produce a standard of unit of work to which a price can be attached and that this price is not a matter for bargaining. If an incentive payment system is to operate successfully, the workers and management must have the same concept of the effort required of a job and the correct rate of payment for it. But it is here that the main difficulties begin to develop. Although time study is used to assess performance, the final result will usually be the outcome of a good deal of hard bargaining. Management as a matter of practice will offer less than is expected and the workers will ask for more. Both sides would compromise a little, they would settle for something between the two, which just because it is a compromise will remain a potential source of trouble and of dispute for the future. It was believed that time study would avoid all this and that the times would be accepted by both sides. But in the actual timing of the job, the time study man finds that he must determine whether the workers are doing the job exactly as they will be when he has gone away, or whether they have introduced additional work elements to lengthen the operation while it is being timed which they will discard as soon as the time has been established. By doing this they will obtain a good rate which will permit them to earn an easy bonus. The time study man, suspecting what is happening, may overcompensate and produce a rate which the management will consider as economic but which the workers will consider to be very tight.

One problem which was highlighted by Shimmin was

that some bonus schemes were so complex that they were just not understood by the workers. She found in one factory using a Bedaux system that a thirteen-page document was needed fully to describe the scheme while in another the description occupied eight pages. A wide variety of allowances to cope with different contingencies partly accounts for the volume of these explanations. Most of the firms expected their supervisors to explain the bonus scheme to new workers, and in all the factories she investigated a complete official version of the payment scheme could be seen by any worker on request and a copy was usually available in each foreman's office. Details of the daily output and the corresponding earnings for individuals were given regularly by each firm so that their workers received knowledge of results, usually one day in arrears. From the workers' point of view, their understanding of and, perhaps more important, satisfaction with the bonus scheme seems to depend largely on whether it made sense to them. This was often a question of how far they could explain to themselves all the contingencies which had occurred. In each factory Shimmin studied, examples could be found of such apparent anomalies as the existence of more favourable bonus rates on some jobs than on others, or instances where there seemed to be no direct relation between extra effort and extra payment. Sometimes this was a matter of history, where the firm was bound by union agreement not to change old and usually loose values because there had been no change in the accepted method of doing the job; in other instances the fault lay in insufficient study of the job itself or in failure to take account of the rates operating on very similar work.

In six factories which Shimmin studied there was great similarity between the types of reason given for liking or disliking wage incentives. Some departmental managers deplored the 'necessity for bribing men to work brought about by full employment', while others felt that a bonus scheme was a better incentive than the fear of losing the job and of being out of work. One or two stressed that financial rewards were not effective substitutes for attempts to improve management–worker relationships as a means of improving productivity. Their reservations included the belief that incentives had a detrimental effect on the quality of the product, doubts were expressed about the social effect, especially the rivalry and jealousy caused by differences in individual earnings.

Supervisors believed that bonus schemes undoubtedly helped production: 'you wouldn't get the work out without it'. But a bonus scheme increased the difficulties of a supervisor in allocating work within his department so as to ensure that there was a fair distribution of tight and loose jobs amongst the workers. However equitably they believed they did this they were always open to charges of favouritism and of messing people about, but the bonus schemes would often enable people to earn so much that 'it just wasn't worth while becoming a foreman'. None of the workers interviewed made any direct reference to the possibility that they could increase their earnings as a result of a bonus system. This was probably because the financial aspect of the scheme was taken for granted. Most of them preferred group bonus believing that there was an absence of friction which would usually result from large individual differences in earnings; there were, however, reservations about conscientious and lazy members of a group receiving the same reward. Workers who did not like bonus felt that it gave a sense of strain, produced bad work, and was hard on the older workers, gave no sense of security, and caused bad feeling and quarrels because of too great a variation in the amount of bonus earnings on different jobs. Upper limits of earnings in some places were very much disliked.

Other points mentioned unfavourably were that on some jobs output was limited by machine speed or other factors which were outside the workers' control and too great a proportion of the wages were bonus; this could cause a loss of earnings if trade declined and a loss of bonus during holiday periods.

Shimmin also reports on three firms that had changed from a direct production bonus to a system of job evaluation with merit rating which they found very satisfactory. They claimed that they obtained increased output, a better quality of work and a smaller and more flexible labour force. But in two other firms which she investigated merit rating had proved to be a source of friction and dislike while a third firm had abandoned it on the grounds that it gave no real measure of an operative's value. She quotes the managing director of a small company: 'This bonus system idea seems to be a form of industrial blackmail – "either we get more money or we don't work so hard". Unfortunately, in modern conditions the firm has to put up with it in order to keep going'. Another firm described bonus schemes as 'just a convenient pistol for labour to hold at management's head.' These views could have been due to the operation of an unsatisfactory bonus system or to a long history of bad industrial relations or prejudice in the firms involved. However, all the firms she interviewed considered that some form of incentive payment was necessary in order to increase the working effort above the customary level obtained with day-rate payment. She reported one group of managers as saying that the basic rate is now regarded as mere 'attendance money' and 'bonus is what you work for'. In some instances bonus schemes were viewed as substitutes for good supervision. There is no doubt that in the early fifties many firms were dangerously inefficient and the operation of incentive payment schemes was considered to be the most immediate remedy.

Merit rating

The main alternative to bonus schemes as a form of individual incentive was merit rating. Although it cropped up occasionally before 1939, its main burgeoning was in the early fifties as an alternative which could be used by those who were becoming disillusioned with bonus schemes. Merit rating was intended to provide a means by which the individual contribution of each worker could be assessed and rewarded. It has been defined by the British Institute of Management as 'a systematic assessment of an employee in terms of the performance, aptitudes and other qualities necessary for the successful carrying out of his job'. There is no uniformity in the rating scales which are used and in the method of using them. Most schemes seem to be adapted to the particular circumstances of the firms which have installed them. It is interesting to note that, although the kind of assessment being employed is a technique in which psychologists have particular expertise, it seems that it is only comparatively rarely that psychologists were asked to assist in devising and installing the merit rating scheme.

Although schemes will obviously vary in detail there are some essential procedures which have to be followed when installing any new scheme. At the outset it is essential that there should be detailed discussion with all the workers involved, with their union representatives and with their supervisors, to ensure that everyone clearly understands just what is being proposed. The full agreement of everyone involved must be sought because without it a scheme is doomed to failure from the start. But first it is necessary to decide how the scheme is going to be run. Decisions will have to be made on the qualities that are to be rated and how they are to be defined, what weighing will be given to each and how the final ratings are to be converted into payment. It will also be necessary to decide who is going to do the rating and how they are going to be trained, and how their ratings are to be cross-checked. There has been a great deal of research on the general problems of the reliability and validity of rating, and anyone introducing a merit rating scheme should be fully aware of the problems involved and the statistical checks which will be required. It is an undoubted prerequisite that a scheme will only stand a chance of being a success in an enterprise where industrial relations are good.

It seems from the published evidence that before a merit rating scheme can be a success there must be someone, preferably someone fairly high in the organization, who is dedicated to making a scheme work. As so often happens all through industry, it seems to be the personality of the men at or near the top which sets the seal on the success of any scheme which aims at motivating individuals either singly or collectively. A number of comments have been made on the adverse effect which the continued growth in size of most organizations is having on the ability of individuals in the management hierarchy to have a close personal influence and an understanding and trusting relationship with the shop floor. Perhaps this is why in 1974–5 industrial relations seem to be just as bad as they could be in many firms.

Lack of a dedicated individual has undoubtedly contributed to the frequent failures of merit rating schemes, and the detailed causes of failures which have been commented on by a number of observers may well stem from this. Such causes are lack of clarity on why the scheme has been introduced in the first place, inefficient rating, inadequate training, lack of support from parts of management and sometimes a complete lack of understanding of the whole procedure. In a paper called 'Seventeen Ways to Mismanage Merit Rating' McMurry (1960) gives a list of things that can cause a scheme to go wrong. It is not surprising that these concentrate on failures in the rating process such as lack of uniformity of standards, the evaluation of subordinates who are known only superficially to the supervisor, unwillingness to use the extremes of a scale, the overweighting of recent occurrences and, perhaps rather cynically, the use of ratings to get rid of subordinates who are felt to be a threat to the supervisor's security! McMurry concludes from his investigation that the ratings which are arrived at are usually unreliable and invalid. 'In many instances the ratings are literally not worth the paper on which they are written.'

Individual schemes have been surveyed by a number of workers who have reported on what they have found. One of these by Davies (1953) may be taken as an example. The firm investigated, situated in the South of England, employed 500 workers on the manufacture of rubber tyres. Most of the jobs were semi-skilled. The merit rating scheme was introduced in 1947 by the managing director, who held that there were four conditions which determined the success of a factory, materials, equipment, technical knowledge and management–worker cooperation. He obtained the first three conditions satisfactorily and then turned his attention to the fourth. He considered that autocratic management was out of date and inefficient and that workers should feel that the factory belonged to them if they are expected to do their best,

Management should keep the workers fully informed of all matters affecting the factory in its trading positions. Each employee should have personal responsibility for his own job and individual merit should be recognized and rewarded.

Extensive consultation took place with the workers on a proposed merit rating scheme; a ballot gave 95 per cent in favour of giving the scheme a trial. Five qualities were rated. 1. Quality and quantity of work. 2. Application. 3. Effort and initiative. 4. Cooperation. 5. Attention to safety, care of tools and material. They were unweighted. Two independent assessments were made, one by the supervisor and the other by the assistant supervisor. The final assessment was made by a panel consisting of the two supervisors, the personnel manager and the works manager. Employees with over three months' service who obtained at least thirty marks were paid an award. Each worker was given his assessment privately and the assessments were regarded as confidential. There were obviously some criticisms, 20 per cent of those interviewed alleged that the points were wrongly allocated, for instance, and nearly a third of the workers said that they did not understand the scheme. In general, however, the scheme was considered to be highly satisfactory both by the management and by the workers. The management thought that it was largely responsible for a rise in output per man, for the reduction of labour costs and the decrease in absence, lateness and a general improvement in morale. Both workers and management also spoke of the scheme as an incentive. A lot of the success could be attributed to the drive of the managing director.

Working groups and output restriction

Output restriction by groups of workers was mentioned in Chapter 2. There is no doubt that it was going on from the earliest times, e.g. Taylor's 'soldiering', and was probably a reaction to the formalization of piece-work with inefficient rate setting which led to rate cutting if operatives were able to earn more than management thought they should. But the idea that rates would be cut, even in firms that had never cut a rate in their whole history, is very persistent, even up to the present time. Pre-1939 employers often actively discouraged the formation of groups by deliberately keeping the workers apart and not providing places where they could meet and talk – other than the toilets; and they could get away with it. But since 1939 the formation and power of groups, particularly of shop stewards' committees, has been very marked, and one of their important activities was often the restriction of output.

Work groups have therefore become a very important industrial phenomenon; perhaps one of the most comprehensive studies of these groups was carried out by Sayles (1958) who said that in research on personnel management inadequate consideration had been given to both parties in the supervisor–subordinate relationship. Most attention seems to have been concentrated on the supervisor. In the not too distant past, management assumed with some justification that each work-group under its supervisor was a team which was dedicated the best interest of the enterprise. These views have now been shattered with reports of restriction of output, anti-management activities of a wide variety, internal bickerings and strife.

The work-group is a primary focus for registering discontent as well as the organizational mechanism for releasing productivity. It is not the isolated individual workman who is responsible for this as many believe. These groups are themselves the product of management decisions which tend to follow the lines of work structure. The technology and organization of the plant are the determinants of the work-group of a variety of types. Changes in supervision may affect changes in the behaviour of the work-group, but the work-group may severely limit a supervisor's range of behaviour and determine what are appropriate or successful supervisory methods.

The objective of Sayles' study was to provide administrators with the means of prediction which would enable them to identify in advance those work-groups which would support or attack management; this would give the administrator a major tactical advantage! Unlike most studies of worker satisfaction, the study did not investigate what the workers thought, but what they did. Thus the investigators were less concerned with what the workers thought they would like to do or might have done. They were concerned with action which was observable.

Sayles identified four types of work group, which ranged from a generally low level and rather disorganized group through a type which was unpredictable, a type which was always doing something, usually to cause trouble, to a group of men who had relatively rare skills who were fairly satisfied with the status quo. It would appear that the kind of group which formed would to a large extent depend on the kind of work which was being done. These four groups were described:

1. Essentially passive, high activity only on special occasions. Individuals working on individual jobs in departments where there is no concentration of employees doing identical jobs; long assembly lines.
2. Unstable, highly demonstrative, volatile. Team operation with all members performing similar tasks; short assembly lines.
3. Persistent self-interest activity which is of a calculated type. Mainly individual operations with some group assembly operations.
4. Self interest causes restraint; basically individual jobs.

The degree of activity, whether tending towards the passive or towards the continuously active, seemed to be influenced by reasonably objective variables such as i) The relative position on the promotional ladder in the plant; ii) Relative size and importance of the group; iii) Similarities of jobs within the group; iv) The degree to which work was indispensable in the functioning of the plant or department; v) The precision with which management could measure work load and pace for the group.

Repetitiveness of the task, the hours of work, the density of the work-force (ratio of men to machines) and sex distribution within the group seemed to be of substantially less importance in explaining behaviour differences.

The highest incidence of grievance activity occurred in

middle-rung group jobs. These are jobs, in pay and prestige, substantially above the starting job in the plant, on which workers feel they have some chance of prospering. There was a lack of any apparent friction over loss of earnings due to the actions of some other group. Hours of work seem to have only a minor impact on the behaviour of work groups.

Continuous struggle over differences between the rates set by management and the rates demanded by employees was one of the sources of wild-cat strikes. Workers with jobs whose production standards can be set unequivocally were less likely to engage in disruption than were those workers whose standards depended upon judgement. Maintenance and craft workers with the greatest degree of freedom to set their own pace were even less likely to cause trouble. Those whose jobs were in many ways relatively routine production operations were likely to be most active. These were the jobs in which management and employees were most likely to differ on a matter of a fair day's work.

When there are uncontrolled technical factors which affect the quality and quantity of output in relation to employee effort and where an incentive plan is involved, a spate of process difficulties can set off a chain reaction. Earnings become less than expected and employees become resentful, frequently focusing their discontent on the work standards which are de-unfair. This resentment probably further diminishes output and management, in reacting to this, places direct pressure on supervision and employees to bring up their output levels. Thus, a sharp downward productivity curve can begin with a modest technical problem and work standard grievances are an additional by-product.

Members of a work-group are expected to adhere to certain standards of output or production which the group as a whole has approved. Within a group of workers physical abilities differ, financial needs differ and also personal standards of what is desirable conduct in the industrial situation differ. On individual jobs there will be informal pressures on rate busters but the determined independent can go it alone to some extent. On team jobs, the output of an individual must be related to the output of the group. The decisions as to how much

101

effort should be expended, what level of earnings is appropriate and how closely the group should adhere to management standards are important ones for the team because individual deviation is almost impossible. Little is known of how groups reach appropriate output standards, but they seem to develop objectives or goals or motivations for two main reasons: as a result of comparisons with the benefits enjoyed by others or as a result of some direct threat to security emanating usually, but not exclusively, from management. For instance, as a result of a bigger share of a team bonus going to some individuals because of, say, a job evaluation system, the less skilled members are reluctant to agree to increase production. They feel that most of the increased earnings will go to the men who are having the bigger share.

Some managements insist that they never succumb to worker pressure. There was no plant investigated by Sayles in which there was not obvious evidence that the degree of unity and strength of a group directly contributed to its ability to win certain concessions.

The belief that getting rid of a few trouble-makers would convert a difficult group into one which is well-behaved was often doomed to failure. Many trouble centres continued to attract trouble-makers; when one was removed another took his place.

A surprising number of companies follow the policy of appointing what they call the 'behind the scenes leader' to a management position, often in the same department. They operate under the assumption that the leader shapes group attitudes, rather than what seems to be more valid reasoning, that the group selects as a leader the kind of person which reflects its own feelings (see B2). Management is often disappointed to find that the new supervisor has no greater control over an unruly group than did the man he replaced. In fact, if he is considered a turn-coat, he may do more poorly because of his change of role.

Individuals may be members of more than one group. In particular they may belong to a social group and a functional group. The social group emerged as the agency which welds the individual to the organization by means of attachment to the immediate and easily perceived face to face group, which provides a source of personal security in an impersonal environment. An administrator who wants to break up these groups because of alleged inefficiency and wasted time on purely social activities is doing a disservice to the organization. It takes skilful leadership to encourage the formation of social groups, at least in organizations undergoing rapid expansion.

Early research in productivity was based on the assumption that internal harmony in a work-group would produce desirable job performance. Increasingly, evidence has suggested that there is little or no relationship between social satisfaction and worker effort.

The functional group will exercise control over output. Without group control, management would be able to utilize individual differences and competition for promotion and greater earnings to establish higher and higher output or performance standards. This would penalize particularly the slower worker and the older employee. It could influence all workers by the cutting of piece-rates where they exist or reduce the number of employees required on the job. Output control is the basic objective of group action as well as an essential element in maintaining group stability. Not only the relation of a member one to another, but the durability of the worker's relation to his job depends on the efficiency of this process. The result is not always unfavourable to management. There are instances on record where the work group has sanctioned increasingly high productivity. Efforts to find a magic formula that would convert low group norms to high group norms have been largely unsuccessful. The evolution of a method of group decision for gaining acceptance for changes in production methods and output standards is a recognition of the potency of group standards. There are instances where groups have resisted management's attempt to reduce quality. When this is happening what possible chance does management have of influencing motivation by the generally accepted methods?

Although in theory relative wage rates, incentive earnings, promotional ladders, lay-off schedules, overtime distribution, quality of working conditions and work loads are equitably distributed amongst work-groups, this is rarely attained in practice because of competition between the work-groups for the available economic rewards. The well-organized work-group will achieve many benefits at the cost of other work-groups, which for one reason or another are unable to exercise sufficient influence. There is an absence of loyalties across group boundaries; workers showed very little sympathy for the problems of fellow employees and would even injure the standing of other employees to improve their own conditions.

An alternative to the observation methods of Sayles is that of joining the work-force and observing what goes on; this approach by Mathewson and by Williams before the war has already been mentioned in Chapter 2. One investigator who also did this was Roy (1952) who worked for a period of eleven months during 1944 to 1945 as a radial drill operator in the machine shop of a machine processing plant. For most of this period Roy kept a diary of his feelings, thoughts, experiences, observations, and of his conversations with his fellow workers which were noted from memory at the end of each day. Thus Roy was able to observe restriction of output at first hand and he came to the conclusion that the main reason for it was a fear of rate cutting. Roy describes in detail how restriction was achieved. The workers seemed mentally to divide jobs into two classes, those which had loose rates and those which had tight rates, keeping production down on loose-rate jobs he describes as a 'quota restriction' with the object of avoiding rate cutting. Limitation of production of tight jobs, which Roy calls 'gold-bricking', was partly an effort to make the rates seem tighter than they actually were and partly a revulsion against having to make too much effort. As a result earnings tended to be bimodal (see A8) and the workers had become very clever in manipulating production on the two different kinds of jobs so that they could maintain their earnings at a reasonable level. From his records Roy was able to state that the time he actually wasted by quota restriction over a six-months' period was 1·39 hours out of every eight-hour working day. During his last two months of employment this rose to just over two hours per day.

So, a situation had developed in which management on the one hand, encouraged by the government, was pressing forward with financial incentives with the object of raising production, whereas the workers on the other hand were forming groups which were becoming increasingly organized which were acting to restrict ouput. Output went up nevertheless. There was very little real evidence for the extent to which improvements had been obtained by the financial inducement *vis à vis* improvements as a result of method changes or improved technology. As time went on management began to realize that some of the steam was going out of the incentive drive while consultants having sucked the incentive orange nearly dry were moving on to other things. It was a time of so-called full employment (there was a lone voice in the wilderness calling it over-employment) and there was a strong desire on the part of management to make sure that his good workers were not seduced away by the firm next door; so they looked around for means of ensuring that the levels of take-home pay (not necessarily of base rates which were becoming uniform) were high enough to ward off any fear of 'poaching'. At the same time the workers while restricting earnings for fear of rate cutting, or whatever, still wanted to earn more money. And so fictitious overtime developed.

The method by which this worked was delightfully simple. The management and individual groups of workers agreed that so much overtime would be worked during the week, the workers having probably kept output down sufficiently to make this overtime necessary; additional production was certainly obtained but the men got paid time-and-a-quarter or time-and-a-half or even double-time for doing work which they could probably easily have done during the normal working day. In order to increase the amount of overtime the unions were pressing nationally for a reduced working week and by this they did not mean working less hours but working less hours on plain time and increasing the number of hours worked on overtime. If management thought of this device as an incentive they must have been sadly disappointed, because there has been no evidence that operatives were working any faster on overtime than they were on plain time; from management's point of view they were merely paying more for something that they ought to have had anyway. The outcome was that unnecessary overtime became consolidated into the fringe benefits which came to be expected from any job. The National Board for Prices and Incomes produced a report in 1970 on hours of work, overtime and shift working in which they came to the conclusion that both overtime and shift work are, in general, viewed with favour by both management and the workers. The report drew attention to the paucity of real information and called for detailed and less subjective assessment of the alleged benefits of overtime, and whether its use represents an efficient utilization of resources.

It seems to be very clear that if somebody earns more than his mates during normal working hours he is considered to be a 'rate buster', but, as the financial return on overtime depends on the time worked, fluctuations in earnings are acceptable. So this remains the only means by which an operative can increase earnings. Both Shepherd and Walker (1958) and Buck and Shimmin (1959) used tax codes as a measure of family and financial responsibility (these terms were used synonymously). The first authors found that for the lower paid the amount of overtime worked increased with increase in family responsibilities; but for the better paid there was little or no relationship. The number of men in this study was 1,000. Buck and Shimmin who studied a sample of seventy men concluded that it was personal needs which determined the amount of overtime worked. 'One of these is his financial responsibility, particularly as it relates to the number of his dependants. The greater his financial responsibility, the more likely is the operative to increase his hours of work by overtime.' Both samples which were studied were paid on a group bonus and this system of payment encourages additional overtime, since it is the only means by which a particular individual can increase his actual earnings.

There can be little doubt that by the end of the 1950s management was beginning to realize that financial incentives, in whatever form they were applied, were, to use an American euphemism, a 'busted flush'. But even before this Whyte (1955) had said that 'the theory of motivation at present generally applied in industry promotes full effort from probably less than 10 per cent of the work force'. And so industry was ready for the next panacea.

Training and productivity bargaining

There had been a certain amount of governmental encouragement during the incentive period and government has become even more involved in the developments which followed. In a sense the training developments were not directly connected with industry's attempts at motivation. The immediate objectives were the encouragement of the training of apprentices and the provision of facilities for training older people in new skills (see E3). To facilitate this industrial training boards were set up, financed by levies on the industries which they served, and which encouraged training by making grants to individual firms and by running their own training schemes. In the early days some of them even supported sandwich course students! Beyond these overt objectives there was an underlying idea that retraining, by giving opportunities for developing into new areas of endeavour, could lead to greater job satisfaction. In addition there was an indirect tie-up with productivity bargaining, a main feature of which was flexibility which in turn meant that individuals might have to learn the skills involved in more than one job.

The Fawley experiment
In most developments there is one example which is not necessarily the first or even the best but which is certainly the most publicized. For productivity bargaining, the show-piece is the Esso Refinery at Fawley just across the water from Southampton.

The early 1960s were undoubtedly a period of change and difficulty. British industry was coming to the end of the 'you've never had it so good' era; rapid technological change was making many old craft skills obsolete; the trade unions were getting steadily better organized and more powerful. On its part management was receiving very little pay-off from its efforts at improving productivity, and was becoming increasingly disillusioned with the separation between pay agreements and the arrangement of work practices on the shop floor. Other restrictive practices, in addition to the restriction of output, were rife. This was particularly true in those industries which had craft unions, the members of whom could see their position and status being challenged as a result of technological change. This was a situation which in some industries, for instance the printing industry, is persisting well into the 1970s.

The main objective, then, of productivity bargaining was that, in return for higher pay, restrictive practices would be abandoned. The major obstacle to this kind of bargaining was that there was an increasing tendency for agreements to be reached on a national level whereas the practices which an employer desired to change were peculiarly local, and national negotiators on the union's side were generally unwilling to commit their individual members in a particular location. But what is a restrictive practice and is it necessarily harmful? A number of attempts have been made to clarify this point and it has become abundantly clear that there is a wide divergence of views even amongst employers; that a practice which is considered restrictive in one plant which may have poor industrial relations may not be regarded as restrictive in another where the industrial relations are good (Zweig, 1951). With this in mind it is pertinent to ask how restrictive practices have arisen. We have already seen that restriction of output seems to have its origin in the savage rate cutting which was the practice at the turn of the century – unfortunately industrial memories are very long indeed; in the same way many other restrictive practices have grown up in order to protect the workers in some way or another from management or to protect particular skills from encroachment by other workers. In either event they are a restriction on the unfettered freedom of management to run their enterprise as they see fit.

With this in mind the Fawley negotiators accepted at the outset that the changing of restrictive practices was the responsibility of the management rather than of the unions, which was the generally accepted view (Flanders, 1964). It does not follow from this that management is in a position to eliminate restrictive practices completely. Anyone who thinks this is possible is living in cloud-cuckoo land. Restrictive practices will always exist to a greater or lesser extent and the important thing is to pick on those, the elimination of which would be of the greatest benefit to the enterprise.

Bearing this in mind the Fawley management put forward a limited number of proposals in July 1960 in what became known as the 'Blue Book'. Basically what they proposed was that there would be drastic cuts in overtime spread over two years with concomitant increases in wage rates to a total of about 40 per cent. In return for this they asked for changes in working practices. These included the relaxation of demarcation lines to give greater inter-craft flexibility, the removal and redeployment of craftsmen's mates, an increase in the amount of shift work, and the elimination of unproductive time allowances. It is doubtful whether management expected all the proposals in the Blue Book to be accepted, but what is important is the realization that management had to convince not only the union officials and the shop stewards but also the individual workers as to the viability of what was being proposed. In addition it was necessary to reassure individuals that the giving up of a protective restrictive practice would not make any difference to their job security. The success of the Fawley management in selling the abandonment of some restrictive practices to their employees set the pattern for most subsequent bargains.

Post-Fawley developments
As Flanders (1964) points out, the important feature of the Fawley experiment was the revision of inefficient working practices as part of a bargain for whose enforcement both the unions and the company accepted responsibility. The unions accepted this responsibility in return for substantial improvements in the wage rates and in the hours of work. Flanders is puzzled why this simple and straightforward procedure was not more widely adopted and suggests that one reason is

'our delusion that productivity can be raised by propaganda'. Throughout the period which we have been reviewing, this propaganda had been promoted by the British Productivity Council with its local productivity committees. It is true that the flow of new ideas and the provision of opportunities for exchange of information had been provided, but the impact on the behaviour of management and the unions in relation to shop-floor activity was meagre. 'The fatal flaw of productivity propaganda is also a source of its attraction: it involves no commitment to act.' The productivity propaganda was aimed primarily at getting other people to do something, the other people usually being the workers on the shop floor. Unlike this propaganda, productivity bargaining *did* involve commitments and so was less attractive.

However, productivity bargaining received a fillip in 1965 when the White Paper on Prices and Incomes Policy allowed increases in pay above norms laid down for money income when there was a direct contribution to increased productivity. As a result there was a big increase in the number of bargains of one sort or another and no doubt both sides to the bargaining felt they were getting something at the expense of the other. The Royal Commission on Trade Unions and Employers' Association of which Lord Donovan was the Chairman had a good deal to say about collective bargaining in general and productivity bargaining in particular. They make the point that before you can bargain on the removal of restrictive practices, you have got to have a definition which will allow such practices to be reliably identified. One gets the impression that they have very little hope that this will actually be possible. As time went on less and less was heard about productivity bargaining, though no doubt it went on quietly in one form or another, but the idea that both parties gave something to the bargain was overtaken by inflation and straightforward salary increase for which nothing was given in return.

In the early 1960s management was becoming increasingly aware that they were coming to the end of the financial incentive road. Some new ideas were required and these would obviously have to be non-financial. Actually, there was no need to develop anything new since virtually every possible approach had already been tried in one form or another before 1939. But memories are short, managers have little time for reading and even less for thinking, so if someone comes along dressing up an old idea with a new name backed by some research of dubious validity and a good publicity organization, there is a very good chance that management will sit up and take notice. It happened when time and motion study was renamed 'work study' which in turn was backed by the ICI organization, and then the idea that the process of breaking down jobs should be reversed and that individuals should assemble larger units of the finished product was renamed 'job enlargement'; and when at the same time the idea that the workers should be given greater responsibility for planning their work was renamed 'job enrichment' with Herzberg as the main protagonist, industry immediately started to explore the possibilities which they offered.

Herzberg's concepts have already been critically discussed in the previous chapter (see p. 72) and will not be repeated here. It will be remembered that his initial investigation was carried out on a comparatively small sample of members of management. The practical application of ideas similar to Herzberg's had already been applied successfully in the 1880s by Ernst Abbé who was no theoretician but a practical man whose future depended on him being right. It is difficult to get any idea of the extent to which jobs are being enlarged or being enriched. It is only when some large company carries out an extensive series of changes that they are written up and published by an academic investigator. Examples of applications on both sides of the Atlantic are available and a sample will be described.

Imperial Chemical Industries

From having been one of the main protagonists of work study and of incentive payments, ICI later switched towards non-financial incentives and the abandonment of various bonus schemes. They freely acknowledge that they were influenced in this by the writings of McGregor and Herzberg. The first group of workers to come off bonus were the process workers who were responsible for running the control rooms of the various chemical plants. Various schemes had been tried to determine how bonus should be paid including the detailed study of eye fixations when standing at a panel of dials, and on the whole they were based on such mundane things as keeping the control room clean. There was a change in company policy and these process workers were taken off the clock and given staff status with an annual salary.

ICI then looked round to see whether the same principle could not be applied elsewhere and to this end there were extensive discussions between the company and the relevant unions, mainly on a productivity bargaining basis that increased flexibility would be exchanged for improvements in pay and conditions. As a result it was decided that some trials would be undertaken in various places. It was agreed that it was common ground '1. That an employee must be employed to the best of his ability for as much of his time as possible. 2. That an employee must be given the status and remuneration which will recognize the importance of his contribution to the company and his acceptance of further responsibility.' With these objectives in mind and in exchange for measures to increase flexibility, all workers to be covered by what became known as the Weekly Staff Agreement would be put on an annual salary but paid weekly. There were eight salary levels which would be settled by local agreement. In addition, as befitted people given staff status, there would be four weeks' notice of termination and also payment for sickness absence; clocking-in was abolished.

One of the places chosen for an experiment was a factory where nylon was spun. Company policy was attaching great importance to the ideas of social scientists, so the document given to all the people involved stressed the need to achieve

112

cooperation and in particular there should be discussions on the idea that money was not the sole motivator. After a series of working parties and shop-floor discussion-groups to thrash out the ways in which the new organization would work, agreements were made with the unions which came into force early in 1968. Just prior to this, social scientists in Bath University had been invited to assess the effects of the changes which were going to be made and it is their account of what happened which is the main published source of information about the experiment (Cotgrove *et al*, 1971). It seems they looked upon the exercise primarily as productivity bargaining which extended into what they called 'job enlargement', but it was actually more an exercise in job enrichment since the nature of the job itself was not actually changed. What was changed apart from the status and payment of the men was that the rule book, a set of rigid procedures which had been established in the days of work study, was abandoned and the men were left to get on with the job as they felt was best. As a result supervision was reduced and much of the responsibility which had formerly been the function of the supervisors was transferred to the operatives who now planned and organized their own work, meal breaks and rest period. Supervision became largely advisory. Due to the additional flexibility which had been part of the agreement, men were able to move around from job to job, even from department to department, in a manner which was determined by the men themselves. A bonus scheme which had been in force for a number of years and which penalized operatives for making mistakes when they produced a lower quality of yarn gave way to a fixed annual salary paid weekly.

From the workers' point of view the scheme seems to have been received with a good deal of scepticism. In spite of careful preparation this scepticism seemed to be expressed in the terms of 'who gets the most out of it?' in money terms: and this was usually believed to be the company. Yet, 62 per cent of a small sample of men interviewed were satisfied with the pay they were getting and only 20 per cent were dissatisfied. It seemed that the comparatively high rate of pay which was offered by the firm was the main reason why many chose to work for the company in spite of the inconvenience of shifts, noise and boredom. Under the new system each knew what his take-home pay was going to be and there was no longer any point in practising output restriction. In spite of the preliminary indoctrination that it is the job which should be the source of positive satisfaction, it would appear that the initial attraction was the increase in pay. The major pay-off seems to have been in terms of decreased boredom rather than 'self-actualization' à la Maslow.

From the firm's point of view the change resulted in higher productivity. At the time the agreement was introduced the plant was working at about 75–80 per cent of capacity. When the agreement was introduced the plant returned to full capacity with an increase of about 20 per cent, but this was eventually achieved with a work-force which was 20 per cent lower than it had been previously. There was a reduction in labour turnover during the first year from a monthly average of 1·36 per cent to 0·43 per cent, but there was a slight increase in absenteeism which may have been due to the improved sickness benefits. Both quality and machine efficiency seem to have improved after the change. On these criteria the experiment could be said to have been successful. Whether it realized management's hope that the men would enter into some kind of Herzbergian understanding of their needs and goals is another matter again. The evidence presented by Cotgrove *et al* is based on the questioning of sixty individuals. The conclusions they draw are expressed in terms of various motivational theories. Sometimes they even draw contradictory conclusions from the same evidence. The trouble with the study of group behaviour such as this is that it masks a wide range of individual differences some of which can be glimpsed from quotations of remarks made in various interviews. While it is likely that some of the workers did get greater satisfaction from greater freedom to organize the work for themselves, it seems evident the job remained a pretty boring one and that the main reason for working there was the high rate of pay. Unfortunately, most of this contradicts theoretical ideas which were one of the main inspirations for this experiment.

At about the same time and depending on the same inspiration and on Herzberg's 'motivators', the jobs of mainly white-collar workers were enriched. A systematic account of each application is given by Paul and Robertson (1970) which in its factual clarity is a pleasure to read after the rather turgid theorizing in the account of Cotgrove *et al*. All the applications were done in the form of experiments using an experimental group and a control group (see A8). Specific changes in job content were made for an experimental group, the job content of a control group remaining unaltered. Also unaltered were 'hygiene' factors such as pay, security, status or working conditions although normal changes in, say, pay were granted to everyone, whichever group they were in, as would have been the case if no experiments were in progress. There was one unusual feature about these experiments, in that the people involved did not know what was going on nor did their immediate supervisors. This was in order to avoid any artificial behaviour such as can occur when people know they are part of an experiment – a 'Hawthorne effect' if you like! In each application the changes were introduced gradually but some of them were so radical that it is a little difficult to see how the individuals in the two groups could fail to be aware that there was a difference between the responsibilities assigned to each. This point is not met in the report.

Five main occupations were experimented with. Salesmen, design engineers, draughtsmen, experimental officers, production and engineering foremen. Less rigorous studies were carried out on tool setters, process operators and some operatives and fitters.

Most of the jobs presented very little opportunity for direct measurement of the effects of the changes. Nevertheless, some ingenious measures were devised. For instance, experimental officers were required to produce monthly reports of their work, and these were assessed by a panel of three managers on the basis of eight criteria. Salesmen were assessed on their sales turnover while foremen were assessed on the way they controlled their budget when responsibility was transferred to them from the managers. Due to these difficulties of measurement the investigators had to fall back on questionnaires to give an index of job satisfaction. There was also a subjective assessment of the effects of the changes.

The changes all followed the well-known pattern of giving more responsibility and less detailed and rigid supervision. Salesmen were now allowed to plan their own calling schedules and they were no longer required to report on the results. They were given authority to make immediate settlement in case of customers' complaints, to deal with faulty or redundant material, and to quote prices within a range of plus or minus 10 per cent of list. The additional freedom and responsibility given to the other groups was much the same. Design engineers were given full authority to spend money within an agreed budget, experimental officers wrote up final reports on research projects for which they had been responsible and were authorized to requisition equipment and materials and similar services. The production and engineering foremen were involved more in planning, and were given complete control of some budgets. The draughtsmen were slightly different as they were all working on one particular project, and the change which was introduced was to attempt to get them together into a group giving them almost complete autonomy to organize their work as they felt best.

The outcome seems to have been universally favourable. Wherever direct measures were available the experimental group performed better than the control group in which no changes had been made. On the measures of job satisfaction the percentage increase of the experimental groups was invariably higher than that of the control groups. The enriched salesmen sold more, the experimental officers wrote better reports and the foremen showed greater saving on their budgets.

From the report one gets the impression of great enthusiasm for the idea of job enrichment in general, and in the ideas of Herzberg in particular. It is interesting therefore to note a brief mention of a problem which upset the study of process operators. It appears that there was some uncertainty about the future of the plant in which the study was being made and, it was claimed, there was a demand for labour from other employers in the district. Over the period of the study labour turnover rose from about 20 per cent per annum to nearer 100 per cent. It appears that pay and, possibly, job security which, according to Herzberg, are not motivators were in fact acting as stronger motivators than was the job enrichment. In other words, people preferred to go to places where there was more money than to stay in an enriched job at less pay.

In spite of this reservation there is no doubt that the changes which had been made in the responsibilities assigned to people in these different occupations had had the effect of improving their work performance and their satisfaction in their work. How long this was likely to remain effective is another matter. This is a question which can be answered to some extent by some American studies.

Some American experiences

A great deal has been published in America, particularly in the 1960s, about work and motivation, but much of the material is theoretical. While some case studies have been reported (e.g. Biggane and Stewart, 1963), carefully documented accounts of job enlargement and job enrichment are comparatively rare. A study by Foulkes (1969) which covers both job enlargement and job enrichment (though the distinction is not made at all clear) has been drawn upon in the following account. Unfortunately the book is rather muddled (one wished for the clarity of Paul and Robertson's account of ICI) so it is not by any means always clear just what happened and what was achieved.

American Telephone and Telegraph Company. Some members of management at ATT became stimulated by the writing of Herzberg. This led to the formulation of what became known as the 'job improvement programme'. This involved giving employees opportunities to do things which they would consider were an achievement, opportunities for recognition associated with that achievement, and opportunities for being given more responsibility. In addition they would be given the chance of advancement to better jobs and for development of their abilities.

One of the first experiments carried out seems to have been

117

with 120 young women whose job was to deal with enquiries from shareholders. Sixteen of them dealt with telephone calls and the remaining 104 answered letters, all using standard language and all checked by a supervisor; their letters were signed by a higher company official. The experiment lasted six months and three-quarters of those who had been there at the beginning remained until the end. The girls were divided into five groups, an experimental group known as the 'achieving' group, a control group, a telephone group and two uncommitted groups. Changes were made only in the achieving group and none of the groups or their immediate supervisors were told that an experiment was taking place.

All the changes involved giving the girls greater responsibility. They could sign their own letters, verification was reduced from 100 to 10 per cent, supervisors no longer saw each incoming letter, each girl could use her own initiative as to the form of the letter and was made responsible for the quality of the reply. Further, the girls themselves were allowed to organize themselves so as to become proficient in particular areas. This method of organization was termed 'vertical loading'. During the course of the experiment the supervisors themselves gave the same responsibility to the telephone group.

In a job such as that chosen, the assessment of the results is not easy and no precise figures are given. On an 'index of shareholder service' all the girls improved but the experimental groups improved the most. They also improved somewhat on an 'index of productivity'. Absenteeism in the experimental group was lower and so was labour turnover which had been very high and was one of the reasons why this body of girls was chosen for the experiment. After the experiment was over more girls proportionally were promoted from the experimental group; 'group morale' had gone up. How this was assessed is not stated; the incidence of personal problems had gone down. The management seemed quite satisfied that what they had done had been a success. They therefore went ahead with a total of eighteen experimental groups covering more than 1,200 employees. Eight of the experiments involved the women who dealt with the company's customers. In view of the high cost of training, the company was very concerned about the high labour turnover. As before, 'achieving' and 'control' groups were used and over the period of the trials labour turnover decreased by approximately one-third in the achieving groups while it increased by about 23 per cent in the control groups. As with the girls dealing with the shareholders, these women were given much greater freedom to use their initiative in dealing with the company's customers. In another experiment twenty-three members of an achieving group had been producing eight units per hour; at the end of the experiment this group had been reduced to fifteen individuals who were then producing thirteen units per hour. In the interim they had completely reorganized the job themselves as also had nineteen individuals on another job who had been working an average of 350 hours of overtime per month. After a while the number of workers had been reduced to sixteen and the overtime to ten hours a month with the volume of work remaining the same.

Naturally, changes of this kind demanded the full collaboration of supervisors and a substantial effort was put into their indoctrination with the Herzberg concepts. Supervisors and managers also met to discuss different ways in which jobs could be improved, and it appears also that discussion meetings were also held with the achieving groups. As time went on, it was left more and more to individual managers in the different divisions to develop as they thought fit; it appears that not every application was a success.

Texas Instruments. As with ATT the activities of Texas Instruments drew their inspiration from Herzberg, but in addition from McGregor's Theory Y. TI's central personnel research unit was staffed by occupational psychologists and there were also psychologists in divisional personnel departments. There were also industrial engineers who were involved in methods improvements and in the setting of standards.

The personnel research unit developed a management training programme on motivation. It was thought to be unrealistic to expect much change from mere attendance on a training course, so the next logical step in the creation of the right climate for management on the Theory Y model was to organize actual applications to particular jobs. Thus the 'meaningful work programme' emerged.

It was traditional that the workers were viewed as a pair of hands and were assigned the 'do' part of a job while management did all the planning, organizing and controlling. To make a job meaningful elements of these three activities were to be transferred to the workers.

An example drawn from an application in one division is related to a complex instrument which was assembled according to the methods prescribed by the industrial engineering department. A standard time for the operation was established at 100 hours. The standard was not known to the group which was taking 138 hours to assemble each unit and this resulted in a loss. An objective of the programme was to make each employee his own industrial engineer; therefore short courses had been run to learn the basic techniques. As a result an industrial engineer became more of a consultant and adviser to the operatives. In order to make use of their knowledge, the supervisor held a meeting at which he asked the operatives to look in detail at the current methods and to suggest improvements. This conference was described as 'a problem-solving, goal-setting session', and the outcome was a rearrangement of the assembly procedure and a target time of eighty-six hours, a reduction of fifty hours per unit. In undertaking the redesign the members of the group were given full access to all information (even information normally considered confidential) and were given all the help they required from the technical experts. When the new methods were put into operation they exceeded even their own target and brought the assembly time down to seventy-five hours. After a time, one of the operatives themselves suggested another meeting resulting in further reorganization and the target was reduced to sixty-five hours. Once again this was exceeded with the actual time coming down to fifty-seven hours and eventually to thirty-two hours. At this second meeting the group told the supervisor that his presence was not required; this caused him some concern but as a consequence of his indoctrination he did not insist on being there.

The account does not tell us what the operatives got out of the reorganization, but as they were paid on an hourly basis presumably there was no financial reward. They must have got something because a member of the personnel research team said that increased motivation could be sensed in the group and absenteeism, turnover, learning time, employee complaints and visits to the health centre were all reduced. On the basis of an attitude survey which was held annually, the operatives appeared to be deriving more satisfaction from their work and there were fewer complaints about such things as food in the canteens. The effect of these and other similar changes made under the meaningful work programme was to hand over to the operatives a number of jobs which were being done previously by different levels of supervision; in other words, the job of the operatives had developed vertically in contrast to job enlargement which involves development horizontally. This does however create problems for the supervisor whose job has changed radically. This applies under any scheme which transfers responsibility from supervision to the individuals actually doing the job. This is looked at in greater detail in a later section.

In his account of TI's work on job enrichment Foulkes (1969) writes of a number of other successful and unsuccessful applications. The lesson which seems to come out most clearly from what happened was the great importance of supervisors of all grades not only being trained to handle the new situations, but also being convinced in the importance of what was being done. In almost every instance the initial meetings which started a study of a particular job were organized and chaired by someone from supervision whose attitude could clearly set the tone for all subsequent efforts. There appeared to be no need for a similar indoctrination for the operatives who seemed to show a natural inclination to take advantage of the opportunities which were being offered. The company believed sincerely in what it was doing, but in the end the success or otherwise of the meaningful work programme depended upon the enthusiasm and attitude of each individual supervisor.

121

The term 'job enlargement' has often been used interchangeably with 'job enrichment' and also with 'job redesign'. This semantic ambiguity seems to have arisen because interpreters of Herzberg's ideas have not been careful to define what was really meant. Job redesign has been with us for a very long time and owes nothing to Herzberg. It has been a matter of common practice for at least three-quarters of a century and is now one of the activities closely associated with ergonomics. Perhaps the best explanation of the differences between job enrichment and job enlargement is that given in the previous section, that the former is expansion of the job vertically whereas the latter is expansion of the job horizontally. This means that job enlargement gives an operative on assembly work more of the task to undertake herself; it is thus the antithesis of job fragmentation, which breaks an assembly down into the smallest practical components, each being undertaken by a different individual. Since job enlargement only involves bringing more of these components together for one operative, it does not imply that the operative has any greater opportunity of planning work or making decisions as is the case with job enrichment. For this reason, job enlargement is looked upon by many as a function of the industrial engineer and, whilst a good deal better than fragmented jobs, is not so good as job enrichment. There is nothing new about job enlargement, it was being practised as a part of good motion study long before Herzberg wore nappies. The objective then was increased efficiency and the outcome was often unsatisfactory.

Published accounts of job enlargement are difficult to find and when results are published they seem to be more concerned with increased production than with assessment of the effects of the changes on the operatives involved. The motives for practising job enlargement are somewhat obscure. On the face of it, the sole objective is greater efficiency, although some may claim that greater interest in the work will increase motivation.

One such application was made during the war. A group

of ATS were changing the nature of the fuse of an anti-aircraft shell, each girl doing one operation and rolling the shells down a long bench; the job was hopelessly unbalanced and appeared to be very inefficient. So a bench was designed using the best motion study principles, which would enable one girl to do the whole job from start to finish. A corporal was instructed in the new method of work and she quickly achieved a rate four times greater than normal. In view of this, additional work stations were constructed and a batch of girls were instructed in the new method of work. So that the girls would not have to leave their places of work, soldiers were laid on to keep the girls supplied with shell and to remove the finished product. After a short trial period when the girls seemed to be doing the job satisfactorily though not particularly quickly, all the fuse changing was transferred to this new set up. But the expected improvement did not materialize; in fact the rate of work was somewhat slower than it had been under the old method. Although these girls were subject to army discipline, a direct order to work faster was out of the question. Instead an attempt was made to find out why output was so low. It transpired that the girls intensely disliked the new set-up because the work stations were too far away from each other to allow them to converse, and even if the work stations had been closer together the amount of concentration required to do the job efficiently would have virtually precluded any conversation. So, the girls were deliberately practising restriction of output in order to force an abandonment of the new method of working. This they achieved because the demand for this nature of shell was such that the lower rate of production could not be tolerated.

So back they went onto their long bench, rolling the rounds down from girl to girl, happily chatting away and singing as the mood took them; but production was much higher than it had been before the girls had been moved to the individual work stations. Could they perhaps have been trying to demonstrate that they could do so well that no alternative method of work was necessary?

This was an exercise in job enlargement, carried out purely to increase output and not to make the job more enjoyable for the girls, which had failed. It failed because the girls did not want to have their job improved; they were perfectly happy as they were and with the opportunities of a social contact which the group method of working gave them.

The utility of job enlargement as a motivator has been questioned. Kilbridge (1961) interviewed assembly line operatives to find out whether they preferred machine-paced to operator-paced conveyor belts (see E4) and larger to smaller job contents. Rather surprisingly the majority had no objection to the machine-pacing; about 51 per cent preferred smaller tasks and only 12 per cent would have preferred to have their tasks larger, the remaining 37 per cent expressed no view either way. An important determining factor, which is not made clear, is how well the jobs were designed and how fast the conveyors were running. It could be argued that these views are simply a resistance to change rather than a genuine dislike of jobs which make the 'operative have to think'. Davis and Canter (1956) give an account of an experiment in which job enlargement was imposed on an assembly line in a pharmaceutical plant with the approval of the company and of the union. The operatives all liked their jobs as they were because it gave them an opportunity for social contact and they did not have to think as they worked. After two years during which each operative did the whole of the assembly task, they were so happy with the new method that they did not wish to go back to the old one; but here again this may be attributed to a resistance to change. A most pertinent comment is that of the Polaroid Corporation's personnel director who is quoted by Foulkes (1969) as saying 'one must beware of social scientists who say some jobs are dull. They may be dull to a college graduate, but not to the people doing the jobs. To find out if a job is dull, one must get out onto the factory floor and interview those who live the life of the job. Some of our female assembly people have high social needs – the work group is very important to them and the job is secondary.' One might take issue with him only on the point of 'going down onto the shop floor and asking questions'. As was pointed out in Chapter 4, if you really want to understand what is going on you should yourself have worked in industry for 'real'. There is not the slightest doubt that to many people social contact in the job is important; job enlargement can seriously interfere with social intercourse.

Job rotation

Job rotation is another technique for increasing motivation by reducing monotony and boredom. There is nothing new about the idea of rotating jobs. Wyatt (1924) reports a laboratory experiment with three subjects and three tasks, which showed a substantial increase in the amount of work done and a reduction in the errors when the subjects had a spell at each of the three jobs during each of the morning and afternoon sessions, as compared with doing one job continuously. The experiment covered a period of six weeks. Wyatt and Frazer (1928) conducted a shop-floor experiment on the manufacture of bicycle chains. One task was machine-paced and the alternative, placing links on two long parallel bars, was self-paced. This alternative job was used during the first half of each morning and afternoon work period. There was a gain in productivity of approximately 6 per cent as compared with the machine-paced job run continuously, the greatest gain being at the end of the working day. A similar experiment was conducted with tobacco-weighing in which one girl cut off and weighed tobacco while the second girl packed it. Three arrangements were tried; working continuously, changing tasks once in each work spell, and changing tasks twice. The first single change showed an 11·2 per cent increase in output, and when the job was changed twice the increase was 13·8 per cent. These experiments were designed primarily to show the effect of changes on output, since in those days they were working on the pretty simple and straightforward assumption that if production went up the job would become more satisfactory for the operatives.

The assumptions underlying attempts at job rotation by the Polaroid Corporation reported by Foulkes (1969) were nothing like so simple. In accordance with the theories which were being publicized in the late 1950s, Edwin Land, President and Director of Research at the company felt that work could be made more meaningful if jobs were rotated. He therefore hired a director and two assistants who evaluated hourly paid jobs to discover which were thought to be routine and which were more interesting and challenging. On the whole, routine jobs were in manufacturing while the challenging jobs were in research and development, quality control, engineering and in the offices. Rotation was therefore arranged between these and routine production jobs. It was not Land's intention that those mastering the more challenging jobs should then apply for a permanent job change.

The director and his staff spent a good deal of time briefing supervisors, foremen and departmental heads and agreeing which jobs could be rotated. It was also necessary to decide how often the rotation should take place; as a general rule a rotation was monthly but on certain intricate assembly jobs it was weekly. It was anticipated that not more than 50 per cent of the jobs in any one department would be rotated. In fact, the number who started rotating in the first year was only seventy-eight although the scheme had been widely publicized to the more than 2,000 employees of the company. These seventy-eight, who were called 'pathfinders' grew to a total of 114 who had entered the scheme by the beginning of 1963, but of these only eighteen were still on rotating jobs at the end of that year. Of the others, fifty-three had been promoted into their more challenging jobs in spite of the fact that this was contrary to what had been expected at the outset, and forty-three had withdrawn from the scheme. In spite of various reasons being advanced to explain what happened, an unbiased observer must conclude that the pathfinder scheme was not an unqualified success; the assumption that given the opportunity, most of the employees would want to participate had proved to be wrong, as also had the assumption that once they started to rotate they would want to continue doing so. In the event, and in spite of the president's clear wish that this should not happen, nearly half the pathfinders ended up full-time in the challenging jobs. If the scheme is looked at from their point of view, it could clearly be said to have been a success and this led on to what was known as a 'job exposure programme' which enabled someone who wished to move to a better job in another part of the company to be exposed to it for a period of between three and six months; during this time the employee could decide whether he liked the job and the supervisor could decide whether he was sufficiently qualified to make a permanent transfer should a vacancy arise. During the exposure period the old job was guaranteed. There was a great deal more support for this scheme than for the pathfinder scheme, and as time went on a high proportion of the exposures were organized on an old-boy basis to the extent that by 1967 virtually all vacancies in more challenging jobs in the laboratory and so on were being filled from the inside. This was aided by the company starting a three-month training programme specifically for people who wished to transfer from production into the laboratory.

Unlike the earlier work of Wyatt, the Polaroid schemes were aimed primarily at improving the lot of the employee. Therefore, it was virtually impossible to quantify what had been achieved and the outcome clearly depended upon the subjective impression of the people involved.

Changing role of supervision

At whatever level changes have been made, be these by way of joint consultation, job enrichment and so on, which have involved individuals taking greater responsibility, there has been an impact on the supervisors who had previously made these decisions. The general impression one gets when reading the accounts of what has happened is that the lower levels of management, that is the levels of management under whatever name immediately above the shop-floor operatives, had received scant consideration in the various reorganizations which had taken place.

In joint consultation, particularly that on the Glacier model, the shop floor has direct access to top management so that far-reaching decisions can be made over the heads of the people in between and without involving them in the consultation process. Jaques (1951) gives a clear account of the problems which arose at Glacier with the middle management level of superintendents and departmental managers. These included such people as the chief inspector, a works superintendent and his five subordinates, chief electrician, foundry manager, stores controller, estimator and so on, some of these being 'works' and some being 'services'. There was apparently some antagonism between the two groups which did not help them to meet the new situation. As Jaques put it, the middle management . . . had become displaced persons. Functional managerial services had been established and these had diminished a superintendent's authority and 'had given rise to intense feelings of loss of status', which was increased by the joint consultatives system which allowed direct contact between the workers and top management. It left the superintendents feeling 'squeezed out'.

An attempt was made to include the superintendents in the consultative machinery by setting up a Superintendents' Committee and giving it a seat on the Works Council. This did not solve the problem and even in some ways made the situation worse, since the superintendents felt they had not only lost part of their authority and status but seemed to have no place in a chain of command in which they could meet and have discussions with their own immediate superiors. The situation changed when one of them was appointed as a new works manager who immediately set up a Works Managers' Meeting which would meet regularly and discuss matters which were related to the way the works were run.

But the problems were not confined to the superintendents. Below them there was what Brown (1960) calls 'the split at the bottom of the executive chain'. At this level also there seems to have been a good deal of worry and uncertainty about the exact role which supervisors were expected to play. Most of the jobs were renamed and terms of reference were more clearly defined, but there was still a gap between the shop-floor workers and their immediate superiors. It would seem that under joint consultation it is easier for top management to tap the resources of the shop floor than it is for those who are in hourly contact with the people involved.

When ICI introduced the weekly staff agreement for their

nylon spinning, they expected their foremen and assistant foremen to act as mediators between management and the operatives; it was their job to put the principles of the new agreement to the shop floor. At the same time they were expected to make radical changes in their own jobs and this was accompanied by a cut of about 30 per cent in the number of supervisory staff. There is nothing in Cotgrove *et al*'s account in 1971 which gives any indication to suggest that there had been any detailed thought given to the effect which the changes would have on the lower level of supervision. It must have been pretty clear to many of the supervisors that by handing on a good deal of technical know-how to the shop-floor operatives, they were in a sense working themselves out of a job. The report quotes a number of things said by the supervisors, and it is fairly clear that some of them were finding the situation quite difficult. The general attitude seems to have been that they were executives, that the decision was made and if they didn't like it they could go and work elsewhere. 'The general impression is that the majority had not only accepted but preferred the new role – *at least of those of the original supervisors who remained*.' (Not italicized in the original.)

Similar problems appear to have arisen in most of the cases which have been reported, and one is left with the impression that while there may have been a good deal of enrichment for the shop floor, there was precious little for the lower levels of management unless they were able completely to change for themselves the nature of their work, since most supervision in the normally accepted sense had become superfluous.

Other motivators

Although most of the incentives used by industry since 1939 have fallen roughly into an overlapping chronological sequence, there are some arrangements which have been tried intermittently both before and after 1939 which belong to no particular period. Some of these, such as the Scanlon Plan (see p. 38), were initiated before 1939 but have had varying amounts of application ever since. Others were expanded since 1939 with a continuing adherence which, in some instances, fluctuates with the economic climate.

Profit sharing

It is doubtful whether even the most enthusiastic protagonist of profit sharing, or as some call it co-partnership, would claim that the appearance in the pay packet once a year or once a month of an additional sum of money acts as a financial incentive and consequently as a motivator. Rather the schemes are thought of as promoting happier relationships between the employer and the worker which gives the worker a stronger sense of participating with management in a joint enterprise. As was mentioned when profit sharing was discussed in Chapter 2, the idea of giving the workers as well as the shareholders a cut of the profits goes back a very long way. As long ago as 1889 an international conference agreed on a definition of profit sharing. Information collected seems to suggest that the incidence of profit sharing is related to the economic climate. When things are going well and there is plenty to distribute, giving part of the surplus to the work-force represents no great hardship. But if times are lean and there is little or nothing to share, management is very loath to give up the very little it has got, and the workers who have come to expect a substantial handout are not going to be content when all they get is a few pennies. All the evidence suggests that profit sharing waxes and wanes with the prevailing economic climate, so the 1930s produced very few schemes whereas the immediate post-war period, when everyone thought they were in on a bonanza, seems to have given profit sharing a new lease of life. These schemes seem to have become so popular in the United States that an organization was set up in 1951 by the Council of Profit Sharing Industries called the Profit Sharing Research Foundation which sponsored the development of schemes by advice and publication.

The idea of profit sharing is delightfully simple, but its execution may lead to all kinds of unpredicted pitfalls. You try to make the workers in a company feel an interest in the company's success by handing them a share of the profit which has accrued from their efforts. Most profit sharing schemes however are simply a shareout superimposed on the existing wage structure, and no attempt is made as would be the case under a Scanlon plan of involving workers in any way in augmenting the size of the cake. Thus most profit sharing schemes probably fail in their objectives and so cease to have any value as motivators; the workers can see no relationship between the hand-out and their own efforts, and they come to expect the hand-out whether there are any profits to share or not.

Writing in 1948, Scanlon rather cynically dismisses the idea that most employers introduce profit sharing with altruistic motives. He sees profit sharing being used 'as a weapon to combat union organization' which, because schemes were usually produced unilaterally by management, failed to develop a sense of partnership or participation and simply raised union antagonism. Alternatively, profit sharing was thought of as a substitute for wage increases – with strings attached. In passing they may note that twenty-five years later Chrysler seems to have had the same idea in the summer of 1975 when they made an offer in lieu of acceding to a wage demand. At the time this Chapter is being written the outcome is still in doubt.

Scanlon goes on to give three examples of profit sharing, two of which failed and one of which was a success. The first of these was in a company with 1,600 employees in the basic steel industry. In 1938 there was a drive to increase union membership which the firm countered with a profit sharing plan which gave their operatives a bigger increase in the pay packet than they could expect to have got through union efforts. As a result the firm paid out nearly one and a quarter million dollars in bonuses over a period of six years for the somewhat 'dubious satisfaction of keeping the union out'. It was a straight payment with no effort being made to produce a sense of partnership or to achieve efficiency to enhance the profit-making possibilities or competitive position of the company. In 1945 the unions launched another attack and, since they were asking for much larger increases than the company was then giving, the union won, but there was a prolonged battle over the status of the profit sharing scheme which ended in a compromise which permitted the scheme to continue, whether or not a share was paid being determined by a formula instead of a decision by the board of directors as had hitherto been the case.

The second case was very similar. In 1941 the unions succeeded in organizing the 1,800 employees of a steel fabricating firm. Negotiations for collective bargaining were dragged on with the company employing lawyers to represent them so that there was no contact between the executives and the union. When no progress was made and the men came out on strike, the company president conducted negotiations himself and the matter was speedily settled. The whole thing was done on such a friendly basis that the union representatives were highly suspicious and wondered what it was all about. Four weeks later they found out when the president informed the union committee that the company had reached a decision to introduce a profit sharing scheme. It seems clear that in this instance the management did not have any ulterior motive but this did not prevent men from believing that it had. The union was only just getting going and the general feeling was that this was an attempt by the company to emasculate the influence of the union. When the president learned of the reception of his plan his immediate reaction was, according to Scanlon, 'to hell with them and the whole damn business. I guess I have been a fool'. From then on no effort was made to make the profit sharing scheme a success. It had been introduced unilaterally without any proper preparation just after a bitter struggle between management and the unions. It did almost the exact opposite to what profit sharing schemes are supposed to achieve in that it had driven management and its workers even further apart.

In the third example given by Scanlon, the company had accepted the union in 1937, and it worked happily without controversy for five years when a joint labour management production committee was set up which amongst other things started the study of profit sharing schemes. As a result of this joint deliberation a scheme was introduced in 1945. Since the scheme had been introduced jointly, its success was not just left to chance but every effort was made by a production committee to improve efficiency and productivity so that there would be a larger profit to be shared. Naturally Scanlon approves very much of this scheme since it is very similar to the schemes which were introduced under his name, the main difference being in the one case it is the total profits which are shared according to a formula, whereas in the Scanlon plan, as we have already seen, it is the savings accruing from increased productivity which are shared.

This final example seemed to spell out the basic requirements for a successful profit sharing scheme. It should not be imposed by management as a kind of handout in lieu of an increase of pay, a handout for which the workers feel that they have no responsibility to contribute. Alternatively, a profit sharing scheme devised and introduced with the collaboration of the work-force which includes arrangements which will enable the workers actively to promote the larger profits in which they will share, should achieve in some measure a breakdown of the 'we-and-they' between management and workers and should motivate the workers to a greater productive effort. But this is not really a financial incentive, since the true motivating factor which can be achieved under this kind of regime can be a feeling of belonging to a firm and a pride in its commercial success. This is not to suggest that the financial rewards are of no importance because obviously they are, but under these sorts of circumstances they are not necessarily of prime importance.

Successes and failures of this kind are not very often written up so we do not know the extent to which other firms have trod in the same path; all that is known is that there are a great many firms that do not stay the course for one reason or another, whereas there are others which have successfully operated profit sharing schemes for a very large number of years.

Status
Denerley (1953) has reported on a large organization that owned many factories in different parts of the country. Since

1928 it has operated an establishment scheme offering workers, 'selected on ground of individual merit, a status and a form of economic security approximating to that of staff'. An 'established worker' had a guaranteed weekly wage at least equivalent to his ordinary time rate, and, if sick or injured, he received this amount (less national insurance benefit) to a maximum of twenty-six weeks in any calendar year. He was also entitled to four weeks' notice of termination of his employment instead of the usual one week, and, in addition, could be granted leave-of-absence on full pay at the discretion of the management. Non-established men who had completed three years' service automatically qualified for sick pay for a maximum of thirteen weeks in any year. All workers who had completed three years of service and were at least twenty-four years old were eligible for establishment, but not more than half of them could be in the established grade at any one time. Selection depended upon the assessment of certain personal qualities and each eligible workman was rated by his local management every six months. Denerley investigated the attitudes towards this scheme between 1949 and 1951. About three-quarters of those who were established gave general approval of the scheme; less than half of those who were unestablished or ineligible made favourable comments upon it. Established men were more satisfied with the firm than were the other two groups. This may have been due to the greater benefits they received from various welfare schemes. Establishment results in a greater feeling of security.

Selection was originally based mainly on subjective assessment of personal policies by the immediate manager, but from 1947 onwards a formal selection procedure was established. Little weight was given to length of service in deciding who should be promoted. The uncertainty of attaining establishment even after a long period of service and the lack of understanding of the scheme would suggest that promotion was too vague and remote to be effective. With a 50 per cent quota there were no obvious differences between the qualifications of the average worker who had just gained promotion and those who had just failed. The subjective nature of assessment admitted bias which was often difficult to detect and measure.

There was no defined standard of performance which would be rewarded by establishment, and the imposition of a rigid quota made prospects of promotion dependent upon performance relative to that of fellow workers. There was more sick leave amongst established workers than there had been when the workers were not established. A union representative is quoted as saying 'many workers think the scheme is not carried out fairly and are opposed to it for that reason. It tends also to separate the workers into two groups, and causes suspicion between one group and another. It is very acceptable on paper but not in practice.' This general criticism by union representatives of the scheme was confirmed in Denerley's interviews. The aims of the scheme were generally not well understood and it seems to have had little effect as a motivator.

Whither motivation?

We have looked at industry's efforts, aided and abetted or hindered by a variety of social scientists, over close on one hundred years to motivate its workers to produce even a reasonable yet alone a high level of productivity. We have seen that the philosophy of the carrot-and-the-stick or System 1 management has been the main means of achieving motivation over most of the period. Why may one ask if the carrot-and-the-stick have worked so well over a very long period (after all they helped to build the pyramids) should there be any need to find some alternative? The reason is pretty clear, as a result of rapid social change the carrot-and-the-stick are working increasingly less well, not only in the highly developed countries but in the developing countries as well. We have seen that people in management have started to realize that some alternative had to be found, and a whole variety of ideas have been tried one after the other; even the carrot on its own has been retained in many situations.

The main characteristic of the last fifteen years in particular has been the extensive theorizing by psychologists with the object of explaining motivated behaviour so as to allow management, hopefully, to be more successful as they move towards System 4. However this according to Drucker (1974) is leading to managers being offered what he calls 'enlightened psychological despotism' in place of the carrot-and-the-stick. He claims that industrial psychologists, most of whom profess allegiance to Theory Y and who use terms such as creativity or self-fulfilment, are attempting to control motivation through psychological manipulation, and this manipulation is based on Theory X assumptions in which the fear of hunger or loss of job or the incentive of material rewards is being replaced by fears of psychological alienation and by the incentive of psychological security. All the different techniques which have been proposed will aid management to manipulate employees in order to achieve higher production, and this says Drucker is 'psychological despotism (which) whether enlightened or not is gross misuse of psychology.'

This may be an over-statement, but there is certainly some truth in it. The majority of people who are theorizing (and this goes for management experts and sociologists as well as psychologists) are often too remote from life as it really is so that situations tend to look simpler to them than they really are. Industry may have got itself into a mess, with management pulling one way and organized labour pulling the other, and both hating each others guts, it may well be looking for help in solving its problems. This help will not be very fruitful so long as it is forgotten that individuals are dealing with individuals, individuals who are all different. Thus we have industry who seem to think that they have only got to find a once-and-for-all panacea and everything will be well, and as we have seen this search for the panacea has led up very odd alleys. Much of the psychological theorizing has not been very much better, in the sense that each theory is presented as if it were the complete answer to the problem. 'Do it this way and all will be well.' There is however a new generation of psychologists who are not interested in developing some startling theory and who do not believe that there is a single solution to the problem of motivation, but only a series of progressive remedies without abandoning what has proved to be useful in the past. This does not mean that it is not profitable to attempt to clarify concepts which are related to these different remedies as they come along, or that there should not be in-plant experimentation and similar activitiy in order to validate particular ideas. What is important is that this should be looked upon as an ongoing process, and should not be fossilized in this or that theory. This new approach is becoming called the 'quality of working life' (Wilson, 1973).

To sum up there would seem to be three important areas which should be taken together when discussing motivation in work. In order of priority these are social, organizational and financial. But this does not imply that one can stand on its own without the others. It is like a three-legged stool, take one away and the whole edifice falls over. The *social* leg implies recognition that every enterprise is a social community and that many people come to work in order to be part of this community, and not just to earn money. The second, *organizational* leg involves worker participation, job enrichment and so on and the third leg, *financial*, implies that everyone in the enterprise gets a share in accordance with their value to the enterprise. The trouble with most of the story that has been told throughout this book is that at one time or another attention has been focused on only one of these three legs to the exclusion of the other two. The financial leg has received a great deal of attention and the organizational leg is being fairly strongly developed. But it is the social leg which is still the weakest and is the least appreciated. The future for motivation in industry will depend on all three being strong.

References and
Name Index

*The numbers in italics following each entry refer to page numbers
within this book.*

Abbé, E. *29, 30, 32, 111*

Argyle, M. (1953) The relay assembly test room in retrospect. *Occupational Psychology* 27: 98. *65*

Bartlett, F. (1953) Psychological criteria of fatigue. In W. F. Floyd and A. T. Welford (eds) *Symposium on Fatigue*. London: Lewis. *79*

Bedaux, C. E. (1921) The Bedaux-unit principle of industrial management. *Journal of Applied Psychology* 5: 119. *12, 35, 36, 37, 91, 93*

Bhatia, N. and Murrell, K. F. H. (1969) An industrial experiment in organized rest pauses. *Human Factors* 11: 167. *79*

Biggane, J. F. and Stewart, P. A. (1963) *Job Enlargement: A Case Study*. Research Series 25; College of Business Administration, State University of Iowa. *117*

Blackler, F. and Williams, R. (1971) People's motives at work. In P. B. Warr (ed.) *Psychology at Work*. Harmondsworth: Penguin. *28, 29, 70, 71, 72*

Brandeis, L. D. *25*

Brown, W. (1960) *Exploration in Management*. London: Heinemann Educational Books. *87 ff., 128*

Brown, W. (1972) *The Earnings Conflict*. London: Pelican. *88, 90*

Buck, L. and Shimmin, S. (1959) Overtime and financial responsibility. *Occupational Psychology*. 33: 137. *106*

Carey, A. (1967) The Hawthorne Studies. A radical criticism. *American Sociological Review* 32: 403. *61, 66, 67*

Chase, S. (1941) What makes the worker want to work. *Reader's Digest 38* (Feb): 15. *62*

Cooley, C. H. (1909) *Social Organization*. New York: Scribner. *46*

Cotgrove, S., Dunham, J. and Vamplew, C. (1971) *The Nylon Spinners*. London: Allen and Unwin. *113 ff., 129*

Currie, R. *15*

Davies, N. M. (1953) A study of a merit rating scheme in a factory. *Occupational Psychology* 27: 57. *97*

Davis, L. E. and Canter, R. R. (1956) Job design research. *Journal of Industrial Engineering* 7: 275. *124*

Denerley, R. A. (1953) Workers' attitudes towards an establishment scheme. *Occupational Psychology* 27: 1. *133, 135*

Drucker, P. F. (1950) *The New Society*. New York: Harper. *75*

Drucker, P. F. (1974) *Management: Tasks, Responsibilities and Practices*. London: Heinemann. *28, 75, 136*

Farmer, E. (1958) Early days in industrial psychology: An auto-biographical note. *Occupational Psychology* 32: 264. *14*

Feldman, H. (1937) *Problems in Labour Relations*. New York: Macmillan. *43*

Flanders, A. (1964) *The Fawley Productivity Agreements*. London: Faber and Faber. *109*

Florence, P. S. *91*

Foulkes, F. K. (1969) *Creating More Meaningful Work*. New York: American Management Association. *117, 127, 124, 125*

Gilbreth, F. and L. *13, 38*

Golden, C. S. (1958) A tribute to Joseph N. Scanlon. In F. G. Lessieur (ed.) *The Scanlon Plan. A Frontier in Labour Management Cooperation*. p. 2. Cambridge, Mass: MIT Press. *39*

Hersey, R. B. *78*

Herzberg, F. (1968) *Work and the Nature of Man*. London: Staples Press. *16, 70, 72 ff., 75, 111, 112, 114, 117, 119, 122*

Herzberg, F., Mausner, B. and Snyderman, B. (1959) *Motivation to Work*. New York: Wiley. *72*

Higham, T. M. (1955) Thirty years of psychology in an industrial firm. *Occupational Psychology* 29: 232. *42*

Hoppock, R. (1935) *Job Satisfaction*. New York: Harper. *45*

House, R. J. and Wigdor, L. A. (1968) Herzberg's dual factor theory of job satisfaction and motivation: A review of evidence and a criticism. *Personnel Psychology* 20: 369. *74*

Jaques, C. (1951) *The Changing Culture of a Factory*. London: Tavistock. *87 ff., 127*

Kelly, J. (1974) *Organizational Behaviour*. Homewood: Irwin. *59, 64, 67, 70, 74*

Kilbridge, M. D. (1961) Do they all want larger jobs? *Supervisory Management*. April: 25. *124*

Kornhauser, A. W. (1939). Analysis of 'class' structure of contemporary American society. In G. W. Hartmann and T. M. Newcomb, (eds) *Industrial Conflict*. New York: Cordon. *71*

Kornhauser, A. W. and Sharp, A. A. (1932) Employee attitudes. *Personality Journal* 10: 393. *45*

Landsberger, H. A. (1958) *Hawthorne Revisited*. Ithaca Cornell University. *45, 66*

LaPiere, R. T. (1934) Attitudes vs. action. *Sociological Forum* 13: 230. *14.*

Lewin, K. *86*

Likert, R. (1961) *New Patterns of Management*. New York: McGraw-Hill. *16, 76*

Likert, R. (1967) *The Human Organization: Its Management and Value*. New York: McGraw-Hill. *76*

139

Lipson, K. A. (1948) *The Economic History of England*, Vol. II. *The Age of Mercantilism*. London: Adam and Charles Black. *19*

Lloyd George, D. *48*

Lytle, C. W. (1938) Recent developments in wage incentives. *Advanced Management 3* (Mar): 79. *44*

Lytle, C. W. (1942) *Wage Incentive Methods*. New York: Ronald Press. *35*

McGregor, D. (1960) *The Human Side of Enterprise*. New York: McGraw-Hill. *16, 39, 75, 76, 112, 119*

McMurry, R. N. (1960) 17 ways to mismanage merit rating. *Business*. March: 82. *97*

Marriot, R. (1968) *Incentive Payment Systems. A Review of Research and Opinion*. (3rd rev. edn) London: Staples Press. *91, 92*

Marrow, A. J., Bowers, D. G. and Seashore, S. E. (1967) *Management by Participation: Creating a Climate for Personal and Organizational Development*. New York: Harper. *86*

Maslow, A. H. (1954) *Motivation and Personality*. New York: Harper. *11, 16, 69, 70, 71, 72, 75, 114*

Maslow, A. H. (1965) *Eupsychian Management*. Homewood: Irwin. *76*

Mathewson, S. B. (1931) *Restriction of Output among Unorganized Workers*. New York: Viking Press. *44, 104*

Mayo, E. (1933) *The Human Problems of an Industrial Civilization*. Graduate School of Business Administration. Harvard University. *42, 55, 57, 61, 62, 63, 65, 66, 90*

Miles, G. H. *55*

Münsterberg. H. (1913) *Psychology and Industrial Efficiency*. Boston: Houghton Mifflin. *14*

Murray, H. A. (1938) *Explorations in Personality*. London: Oxford University Press. *70*

Murrell, F. *41*

Murrell, K. F. H. (1962) Operator variability and its industrial consequences. *International Journal of Production Research 1* (*3*): 39. *78, 79*

Murrell, K. F. H. and Forsaith, B. (1963) Laboratory studies of repetitive work II: Results from two subjects. *International Journal of Production Research 2*: 247. *79*

Murrell, K. F. H. (1965) Le concept de fatigue une réalité ou une gêne? *Bulletin du CERP 14*: 103. *79*

Murrell, K. F. H. (1971) Industrial work rhythms. In W. P. Colquhoun (ed.) *Biological Rhythms and Human Performance*. Ch. 12. London: Academic Press. *23, 37, 63, 85*

Murrell, K. F. H. (1974) Performance rating as a subjective judgement. *Applied Ergonomics 5*: 201. *36*

Myers, C. S. (1926) *Industrial Psychology in Great Britain*. London: Jonathan Cape. *14, 45, 54, 55*

Neal, L. (1971) Future trends in industrial relations. *Occupational Psychology 45*: 167. *17*

NIIP, (1952) *Joint Consultation in British industry*. London: Staples Press. *85*

Patterson, (1964) Unitary theory of motivation and its counselling implications. *Individual Psychology 20*: 17. *11*

Paul, W. J. and Robertson, K. B. (1970) *Job Enrichment and Employee Motivation*. London: Gower Press. *74, 115, 117*

Roethisberger, F. J. and Dickson, W. J. (1939) *Management and the Worker*. Cambridge, Mass: Harvard University Press. *13, 55, 59, 60, 62, 64, 65, 66*

Ross, E. H. (1908) *Social Psychology*. New York: Macmillan. *46*

Roy, D. (1952) Quota restrictions and gold-bricking in a machine shop. *American Journal of Sociology* 57: 427. *104*

Rowntree, S. *41*

Royal Commission on Trade Unions and Employers Associations (1968) The Donovan Report. London: H.M.S.O. *110*

Sayles, L. (1958) *Behaviour of Industrial Work Groups*. New York: Wiley. *99 ff.*

Scanlon, J. (1948) Profit sharing under collective bargaining: Three case studies. *Industrial Labour Relations Review* (October 1948). *27, 38 ff., 129, 131, 132*

Shaw, A. *38*

Shepherd, R. D. and Walker, J. (1958) Absence from work in relation to wage level and family responsibility. *British Journal of Industrial Medicine* 15: 52. *106*

Shimmin, S. (1955) Incentives. *Occupational Psychology* 29: 240. *92*

Shimmin, Sylvia, (1959) *Payment by Results: A Psychological Investigation*. London: Staples Press. *92 ff.*

Strong, E. V. (1934) Aptitudes versus attitudes in vocational guidance. *Journal of Applied Psychology* 18: 501. *85*

Taylor, F. W. (1895) A piece-rate system, being a step towards partial solution of labor problems. *Transactions of the American Society of Mechanical Engineers*, 16: 856. *12, 18, 20 ff., 29, 30, 32, 33, 34, 35, 37, 38, 42, 48, 98*

Taylor, F. W. (1947) *Scientific Management*. New York: Harper. *27*

Thomas, W. I. (1904) The province of social psychology. *American Journal of Sociology* 10: 445. *46*

Uhrbrock, R. S. (1935) *A Psychologist Looks at Wage Incentive Methods*. New York: American Management Association. *44*

Vernon, H. M. (1921) *Industrial Fatigue and Efficiency*. London: Routledge. *48*

Viteles, M. S. (1932) *Industrial Psychology*. London: Jonathan Cape. *45, 65*

Viteles, M. S. (1954) *Motivation and Morale in Industry*. London: Staples Press. *19, 59, 65, 70, 91*

Vroom, V. H. (1964) *Work and Motivation*. New York: Wiley. *11, 16, 74*

Wade, M. (1973) *Flexible Working Hours in Practice*. London: Gower Press. *82*

Watkins, G. S. (1929) *Labour Problems*. New York: Thomas Crowell. *44*

Watson, J. J. *30, 32*

Welsh, H. J. *55*

Whitehead, T. N. *55*

Whyte, W. F. (1955) *Money and Motivation: An Analysis of Incentives in Industry*. New York: Harper. *107*

Williams, W. (1925a) *Full Up and Fed Up*. New York: Scribner. *45, 104*

Williams, W. (1925b) *Main Springs of Men*. New York: Scribner. *45*

Wilson, N. A. B. (1973) *On the Quality of Working Life*. Manpower Papers No. 7. London: H.M.S.O. *137*

Wyatt, S. (1924) *On the Extent and Variety in Repetitive Work. Pt. B. The Effect of Changes in Activity*. IFRB Rept. No. 26. London: H.M.S.O. *49, 78, 125, 127*

Wyatt, S. (1934) *Incentives in Repetitive Work*. I.H.R.B. Rept. No. 69. London: H.M.S.O. *49*

Wyatt, S. and Frazer, J. A. (1928) *The Comparative Effect of Variety and Uniformity in Work*. IFRB Rept. No. 52. London: H.M.S.O. *125*

Wyatt, S. and Langdon, J. N. (1937) *Fatigue and Boredom in Repetitive Work*. IHRB Rept. No. 77. London: HMSO. *48*

Zeiss, K. *29*

Zweig, F. (1951) *Productivity and the Trade Unions*. Oxford: Blackwell. *108*

Subject Index